PRAISE FOR *THE WELL-BEHAVED CHILD*

"John's done it again! This may be his best book yet!"

Kevin Leman

Author, *Have a New Kid by Friday*

"In a day when many so-called 'experts' are dispensing politically correct parenting advice that is doomed to fail, John Rosemond is truly a breath of fresh air. His common-sense approach to childrearing has been used successfully by millions of moms and dads—because it actually works! If your desire is to become a more confident, effective, loving parent, I urge you to read *The Well-Behaved Child*."

Bill Maier, PsyD

Psychologist in Residence,

Focus on the Family

"What mom hasn't wanted an instruction manual to walk her through how to navigate the ups and downs of raising kids? If you've ever wanted to get intentional with your parenting, be equipped to maintain your cool, show your kids who is really in charge, and raise kids who become well-adjusted and respectful adults, this is a must read. I think this book should be required reading for every parent!"

Lysa TerKeurst,

Mom to five; President, Proverbs 31 Ministries; Award-winning author of

12 books, including *Becoming More Than a Good Bible Study Girl*

"When people seek guidance from me on raising children, and especially discipline principles, I give them two words: *John Rosemond*. John is America's family expert. He reminds parents that we are in charge. His advice is a no-nonsense approach to raising well-adjusted kids (and parents!). Read this book, follow the advice, and you will have a parenting plan that works."

Jim Burns PhD

President, HomeWord

Author, *Confident Parenting*

"This book is a veritable *treasure chest* for parents and professionals alike, conveying in powerful and easily understood ways the principles for raising children to become good citizens—along with practical methods for application. As a practicing pediatrician with a heavy emphasis on managing common childhood behavior problems following eleven years in academic pediatrics, teaching parents these principles and using the methods described have led to rapid and enduring resolution of behaviors qualifying as ADHD, ODD, and EOBD (early onset childhood bipolar disorder) for many children. Parents who are enabled to avoid pressures to put their child on powerful medication—or stop giving medications already prescribed—intuitively embrace these ideas almost without exception. Their responses have become the most rewarding and fulfilling of my career in pediatrics during the past few years of taking this common-sensical, non-medical, wellness approach."

DuBose Ravenel, MD, FAAP, FCP
Coauthor, *The Diseasing of America's Children*
Cornerstone Pediatrics
High Point, North Carolina

THE
WELL-BEHAVED
CHILD

Other Books by John Rosemond

Parenting by the Book

The Diseasing of America's Children

Making the "Terrible" Twos Terrific

Teen-Proofing

A Family of Value

Because I Said So!

The New Six-Point Plan for Raising Happy, Healthy Children

THE
WELL-BEHAVED
CHILD

Discipline That *REALLY* Works!

JOHN ROSEMOND

THOMAS NELSON
Since 1798

NASHVILLE   DALLAS   MEXICO CITY   RIO DE JANEIRO   BEIJING

Published in Nashville, Tennessee, by Thomas Nelson. Thomas Nelson is a registered trademark of Thomas Nelson, Inc.

Thomas Nelson, Inc. titles may be purchased in bulk for educational, business, fund-raising, or sales promotional use. For information, please e-mail SpecialMarkets@thomasnelson.com.

All Scripture quotations, unless otherwise indicated, are taken from The HOLY BIBLE, NEW INTERNATIONAL VERSION®. © 1973, 1978, 1984 by International Bible Society. Used by permission of Zondervan Publishing House. All rights reserved.

Scripture references marked NKJV are from THE NEW KING JAMES VERSION. © 1982 by Thomas Nelson, Inc. Used by permission. All rights reserved.

Published in association with The Steve Laube Agency.

Library of Congress Cataloging-in-Publication Data

Rosemond, John K., 1947–
    The well-behaved child : discipline that really works! / John Rosemond.
        p. cm.
    Includes bibliographical references.
    ISBN 978-0-7852-2904-9 (hbk.)
    1. Discipline of children. I. Title.
    HQ770.4.R674 2009
    649'.64—dc22

2009023462

Printed in the United States of America

09 10 11 12 13 QW 6 5 4 3 2

To Willie:
Don Gibson, and later Ray Charles, said it best:
"I can't stop lovin' you."
La Chaim!

. . . And to all the parents who've shared so generously and trustingly with me over the years, and taught me so very much in the process.

. . . And to God, the Father, Son, and Holy Spirit, who makes all things possible and without Whom nothing is possible!

No discipline seems pleasant at the time, but painful.
Later on, however, it produces a harvest of righteousness
and peace for those who have been trained by it.

—HEBREWS 12:11

Train up a child in the way he should go,
And when he is old he will not depart from it.

—PROVERBS 22:6 NKJV

Contents

Read This First!

(Because I Said So!)

Never in any culture at any time has parenting been more stressful than it is in today's America. The problems began in the late 1960s, when parents stopped taking their cues from their elders and began following the advice of people like me: psychologists and other mental health professionals. This book, like my other books, is an attempt to right that generally wrong counsel. The discipline of children is not difficult. It's a relatively simple matter, in fact. I intend to prove that to you. You can be the parent you want to be. You can have well-behaved children.

Without a doubt, the single biggest source of frustration, stress, anxiety, confusion, resentment, and guilt for today's parents is their children's misbehavior. They are in the dark as to why it occurs, unclear as to how to deal with it, confused by the cacophony of disciplinary strategies that compete for their attention in the parenting marketplace, occasionally angered by it, and beset by nagging internal voices that tell them it's their fault in the first place. The resulting general disciplinary ineffectiveness has spawned an ever-worsening misbehavior epidemic, the symptoms of which would have shocked our great-grandparents.

Not only are incidences of misbehavior increasing, but the problems themselves are escalating in seriousness. Fifty years ago, it was unheard-of for a child who had reached age three to hit his parents; today, it is not unusual to find children five and six years of age who are hitting their parents (usually their mothers) on a regular basis. Biting is another example of culturewide disciplinary decay. No one my age remembers children who bit. Since permanent memory generally develops around the third birthday, that means the first wave of baby boomer kids had stopped biting—not all that unusual for toddlers—by that time. Today, kids come to kindergarten still expressing the will to dominate with their teeth. Fifty years ago, children were mischievous, but the rare child was belligerently defiant; today, the once-rare insolent child is everywhere. Fifty years ago, tantrums had stopped by age three. Today, it's not at all unusual for children still to be having major emotional meltdowns well into their elementary school years. Fifty years ago, children were expected to do their own homework, and notwithstanding the occasional purposeful lapse, they did. Today, many children will not do their homework unless their parents sit with them, driving the process to a belated conclusion. And the list goes on and on and on.

No wonder parents feel overwhelmed and are turning, in growing numbers, to professionals for relief. Unfortunately, the relief in question often takes the form, not of actual solutions, but of *nouveau* (i.e., worthless) advice and unproven therapies that spin everyone's wheels or of drugs that solve nothing and simply reduce the misbehavior in question to manageable levels.

In the course of a typical year, I spend most of my time on the road, talking to parent and professional audiences across the USA. I daresay I talk face-to-face with more parents than anyone else in my field, and most of these conversations concern behavior problems. On top of this, I answer hundreds of questions a year submitted by parents through the members' side of my Web site (www.rosemond.com). More than 90 percent of these questions constitute pleas from parents (and an ever-increasing number of custodial grandparents) for disciplinary solutions. The desperation parents feel when it comes to the issue of discipline is also reflected in the fact that my two most well-attended talks are "Parenting the Strong-Willed Child" and "The Keys to Effective Discipline."

In the 1980s, I began putting together a teaching workshop to train parents in the fundamental principles of effective discipline and to provide them with user-friendly discipline strategies that were adaptable to a broad range of misbehaviors. Over the years, through my private practice and the work I do with parents through my Web site and workshops, parent coaching practice, and continuing consultations with parents in other contexts, I've developed, field-tested, and refined a set of approaches to discipline problems that, as the subtitle of this book proclaims, "*REALLY* works!" These are simple, effective, down-to-earth strategies that are easy to implement, easy to manage, and easy to supplement if the need arises. They are adaptable to a broad spectrum of family situations and problem scenarios.

Furthermore, unlike so many discipline tools out there, these strategies don't work for a while and then, when the novelty wears off, stop working. Assuming parents work at them, they work, and they keep on working to not just control misbehavior but to virtually eliminate it. Testimony after testimony from parents around the USA attests to great improvements in child behavior, family communication, parent-child affection, and the overall quality of family life following the implementation of these practical approaches.

Parents Say It Works!

"Your ticket system transformed our discipline and transformed our family!"

In effect, *The Well-Behaved Child: Discipline That* REALLY *Works!* is a workshop-in-a-book. I will take you through a step-by-step program that is easy to understand, implement, and manage. The principles and the procedures have proven effectiveness with a wide range of discipline problems. For example, the same system used to solve the problem of misbehavior in public places can, with a few simple tweaks, be used to virtually eliminate disruptive sibling conflict. But the solutions presented by no means suppose that "one size fits all" (another feature of *all* the other discipline programs in the market); I recognize that what works with Billy may not work with Bubba and what feels comfortable to Billy's parents (or fit their lifestyle) may not feel comfortable to Bubba's. For any given problem or set of problems, parents will be able to choose from among a variety of strategies, all based on the same set of simple principles, and all equally effective.

Some parents may have the urge to go straight to the section that deals with the most vexing problem they are having with their child. If you are one of the parents in question, and you have even read this far, I encourage you to fight the urge to run straight to the dessert counter. Again, this is a workshop-in-a-book. As such, the material is organized so that every section builds on concepts developed previously. Taking things out of order invites the possibility that, in your impatience, you will create more problems than you solve.

Today's parents believe that correct methods, correctly used, will solve discipline problems. Underlying that is the belief that behavior modification—the manipulation of reward and punishment—works with human beings as well as it works with rats, pigeons, and dogs. As we will discover, it does not. Correct methods, correctly used, will bring about temporary improvements in some behavior problems some of the time, but will not make a dent in most behavior problems most of the time. Nonetheless, and as you might have already noticed, chapter 3 of this book is replete with discipline methods (and directions on how to use them correctly). I repeat: chapter 3. If correcting behavior was a simple matter of methods alone, I'd have written chapter 3 only and published it as a booklet. Chapter 3 is about *doing* the right thing. It consists of disciplinary recipes, if you will. But any good cook will tell you that even the best of recipes does not guarantee a savory dish. Before a person can turn a recipe into something worth eating, he must learn *how* to cook, and competent cooking is largely a matter of attitude, panache, *élan*, style. And so it is with disciplining a child. The methods I've detailed in chapter 3 are going to fall flat without the right attitude, which is described in chapters 1 and 2. That is why it's important that you not read this book out of order.

In chapter 4, I reveal the top seven behavior problems of all time and how to deal successfully with them.[1]

In chapter 5, I describe how parents I've worked with have succeeded at banishing some very strange, unusual, and downright weird behavior problems from their households—like the little girl who pulled out her hair and the boy who itched himself incessantly. Some kids do weird things. They don't necessarily do these things because they have psychological problems. More often than not, they behave in strange, unusual, and downright weird ways just because (a) they are children and (b) they are human. People who think they can explain these sorts of things are kidding themselves (and fooling other people in the process). The important thing is not to explain them but to help children stop doing them and join the real world.

Now, it's important to note that I've focused most of my strategies in this book on disciplining children between the ages of three and thirteen, what I refer to as the "Decade of Discipline." The approach to discipline I describe herein is only possible with a child who is (a) paying pretty good attention to his or her parents, (b) tuned in to parental approval, and (c) capable of remembering consequences. Typically, those abilities begin emerging around the second birthday and are not adequately established until age three. Despite this limitation, however, parents can lay good disciplinary *foundations* prior to age two and can begin making significant disciplinary inroads between the second and third birthdays. I've already written a book on those very subjects—*Making the "Terrible" Twos Terrific!*[2] This book picks up where that book left off.

Likewise, a discipline strategy that works with a child of, say, seven will probably not work with a teen and may even make matters worse. The principles I set forth in chapter 2 still apply, but the approaches described in chapter 3 may well backfire with that age child. I've written a book on how to parent children ages thirteen and older—*Teen-Proofing*—in which I describe the unique considerations one must bring to that ball game.[3]

One final thought before we get started: In the 1960s and 1970s, we stopped listening to our elders tell us how to raise kids and began listening instead to people with capital letters after their names—people like me. Although I love what I do and I am greatly blessed every time a parent tells me that my advice helped them resolve a problem, I think it's more than a bit sad that today's parents are reading books instead of listening to their elders. I comfort myself with the fact that I officially became an "elder" on November 25, 2007 (my sixtieth birthday). I am further comforted by the fact that people a generation older than myself tell me my advice is very consistent with the manner in which they approached the raising of children, before it became known as "parenting." But then, as we are told, there is nothing new under the sun.

CHAPTER ONE

Why Children Misbehave

This book exists because children misbehave—not *some* children, *all* children. Some are blatant and loud about it, and some are subtle and quiet about it, but they *all* misbehave. It would be one thing if their misbehavior were the result of ignorance, of not knowing that they were misbehaving, but children misbehave even when they know what they're doing is wrong. It is therefore necessary, at the outset, to explain the "why?" behind this ever-present feature of their nature. In other words, for you to discipline your child successfully, you must first understand what makes children "tick." That makes sense, doesn't it? After all, you can't train a dog successfully without knowing what makes dogs tick.

If asked "Why do children, all children, misbehave?" most psychologists (of which I am one) would employ one or more of the following words or phrases: unresolved issues (or unresolved conflicts), anxiety, stress, conflicting messages, cries for help or attention, trauma, post-traumatic, power struggles, chemical imbalances, and genes. Nope. Some of those words may help us understand why four-year-old Jonathan Schmedly-Jones of Omaha refuses to obey his parents, but

1

none of those words explains why *all* children misbehave, and deliberately so. As it turns out, the explanation is simple—so simple that most psychologists never think of it (and if they did think of it, they would deny they thought of it): children are bad. They do not misbehave because their innocent nature has been corrupted by bad parenting or chemical imbalances or rogue genes or "issues" (although, and again, explanations of that sort may apply in some small way to some relatively small number of children). Children misbehave because they are *bad*, and the sooner parents understand and accept this, the better for them and the better also for their children. The incontrovertible badness of children is why it takes most of two decades to fully socialize them. Their badness is the reason for this book.

I fully realize that kicking things off with the assertion that children are not good by nature will surprise, if not shock, many parents. It would not have shocked parents of bygone generations, but then those were parents whose common sense had not been drowned in a deluge of postmodern psychobabble. When their children began to misbehave, they were not surprised; rather, they fully expected it. They understood that good parenting, no matter how good, did not guarantee good behavior. Because their child-rearing feet were planted firmly on the solid ground of common sense, bygone parents were able to maintain their sense of parenting balance and respond to bad behavior authoritatively, with generally calm purpose.

According to a continuing poll I take with my numerous parent audiences per year, today's parents are far, far more likely than were their parents to yell at their children. This relatively recent upsurge in parental yelling is a sign that parents have lost confidence in themselves. That has happened, I submit, because parents have been listening to professional voices for more than forty years instead of listening to their elders. Reclaiming that confidence—that sense of balance and authority— requires a restoration of common sense where children are concerned, and the cornerstone of parental common sense is the understanding that in any given situation, a child is inclined by nature to do the wrong thing, the *self*-serving thing, the bad thing. Parents who refuse to accept that are in for a rough ride.

Parenting Axiom One

No matter how good a parent you are, your child is still capable,
on any given day, of doing something despicable, disgusting, and depraved.

Parenting Axiom Two

Parents who accept Parenting Axiom One will have a
more relaxed, happy, and playful parenthood than parents who
do not. Their children will also be much easier to discipline.

A child's badness awakens from the slumber of infancy sometime during the second year of life. Parents put a sweet little eighteen-month-old angel—a child who's never given them a moment's trouble—to sleep one night and the Demon Spawn of Satan wakes up the next morning, raging. When she's picked up, she rages to be put down. When she's put down, she rages to be picked up. When picked up again, she bites or scratches. She rages for milk, but when given milk she knocks it to the floor and rages for orange juice. Given the orange juice, she rages for milk. And so it goes.

The mentality of the awakened human being, otherwise known as "a toddler," consists of five related beliefs:

1. What I want, I deserve to have.
2. Because I deserve what I want, the ends justify the means.
3. No one has a right to deny me or stand in my way.

4. The only valid rules are those that I make.

5. The rules, even ones that I make, do not apply to me.

That same set of beliefs is also shared by criminals and dictators, and indeed, the toddler is at turns a criminal-in-the-making and a tyrant-in-the-offing. As such, it is a measure of God's grace and mercy that, of all the ambulatory species on the planet, human beings do not to grow to full size in one or two years. It's one thing to deal with a tantrum in a toddler who is twenty-four inches tall and weighs the same number of pounds. It would be quite another to deal with a tantrum from a two-year-old who was five feet ten and weighed 160 pounds. America doesn't have enough emergency rooms!

One does not need to teach badness to a toddler. They are factories of antisocial tendencies. As soon as they learn to talk, they begin to lie. They assault people who don't give in to their demands. They steal other people's property. (I said this to a group of parents once, and someone rejoined that this age child does not know he or she is stealing. They take things because they are curious, she said, to which I simply asked, "Then why do they hide them and deny they've taken them?" End of discussion.)

No psychological paradigm exists that will explain the antisocial behavior of the toddler. How is it that a twenty-month-old who has never seen an act of violence or heard one described, who has been the recipient of nothing but love, slaps his mother across the face one day because she has told him he cannot have a cookie? How is it that a two-year-old who has been treated generously by everyone in his life is malevolently selfish? Why does a toddler who has never been screamed at scream at his parents when they do not obey him? I am describing here not just the behavior of *two* toddlers, but the behavior of *all* toddlers. I repeat: toddlers are criminals-in-the-making. Behavioral theory—which posits that all behavior is learned—does not suffice to explain their misbehavior. Humanistic psychology says human beings are by nature good, so we can toss that out the window with a big guffaw. Not one of Freud's notions concerning the nature of human beings rises to the occasion.

The only explanation that fits is that humans are born this way; it is their nature to be cruel, to be criminal, to be Lords and Lordettes of the Flies.

Parents who understand that badness is the natural state of the child will not be knocked off balance when the Demon Spawn awakens. They will simply look at one another and shrug their shoulders, realizing and accepting that the honeymoon is over. Prior to this sea change, they were merely caretakers, concerned primarily with making their child feel welcome and wanted, as well as keeping her healthy, comfortable, and safe from harm. Now, however, their real job—the task of *raising* Master or Mistress Bad-to-the-Bone out of a state of narcissistic savagery into a state of prosocial civility—begins. From this point on, parents are exorcists. Their job is to exorcise those demons that can be pried loose and help their child learn to control those that refuse to let go. The end result is a child who willingly walks the straight and narrow path toward good citizenship.

"She Doesn't Really Mean It!"

I received a letter from the exasperated mother of a three-year-old girl whom Mom described as "constantly in motion, gets into everything, won't stay in her bed at night, won't accept 'No' for an answer . . ." and so on. In the midst of her description of this little hellion, Mom wrote: "I know she's well intentioned."

I wrote back to this mother: "Well intentioned? No, your daughter is not well intentioned. She *intends* to have it her way, she *intends* to prove she can outlast you, and she *intends* to prove she runs the show. She is doing what she is doing with bad intention, and you will not be able to discipline her properly until you stop thinking she is innocent and making excuses for her."

I never heard back from her, so I assume the child is still well intentioned.

Some children submit to their exorcisms more easily than others. "Why?" is anyone's best guess. These days, children who cling to their demons for all they're worth are usually called "strong willed." But *all* children are strong willed. They all want their own way, all of the time. So do you. So do I. (You and I, however, have accepted that [a] we can't always have our way, and [b] it's sometimes better in the long run to let someone else have *their* way.) Some children, as is the case with some adults, simply go about trying to get their own way more subtly, more cleverly than others. They charm adults into giving them their way. To charm means to cast a spell, and casting spells is evil. These very charming kids, therefore, are just as bad as children who, lacking the talent of spell-casting, go about trying to get their way in clumsier fashion.

Exorcising a child's demons requires punishment. The operative principle is simple: *when a child does something bad, the child should feel bad about it.* Unfortunately, when they do bad things, children do not feel bad on their own. A conscience does not fully develop until early adolescence, at best. Therefore, when they do bad things, children need other people, adults, to help them feel bad. That requires punishment. What a wonderful world it would be if that weren't the case! What a wonderful world it would be if children could be talked out of misbehaving!

In the 1960s, mental health professionals decided that reasoning with children was possible. Where they came up with that idea is beyond me, but they did. Lots of dumb ideas emerged during the 1960s, most of which have fallen by the wayside. This particular bad idea has proven especially stubborn, however. Today, nearly every issue of every parenting magazine contains an article suggesting that children can be reasoned with. The truth is they cannot be, period. The phrase "reasoning with a child" is an oxymoron, which means only morons believe it's possible. When a child is old enough to be successfully reasoned with, he is no longer a child. He's ready to leave home—and he should.

Adele Faber, the coauthor of *How to Talk So Kids Will Listen & Listen So Kids Will Talk* (can you tell that Ms. Faber and I are not on the same page?), once accused me of being "hung up" on punishing children.[1] That's the equivalent of saying that a successful gardener is "hung up" on yanking weeds out of her garden. Punishment is every bit as necessary to raising a well-behaved child as weeding is to growing a successful garden.

The analogy works at several levels:

- Gardeners do not enjoy weeding; they simply accept that it must be done. Likewise, parents should not enjoy punishing; they should simply accept that it must be done.
- If not pulled, weeds will eventually choke the good plants and take over. Like weeds, bad behavior is more powerful, more insistent, more aggressive, more tenacious, and more insidious, than good behavior. It has to go.
- A garden cannot weed itself, and children cannot discipline themselves (until they have been successfully disciplined).
- Any experienced gardener knows that the most critical time to weed is when the garden is young. The more effectively one weeds when the garden is young, the less one will have to weed later. The same is true as regards the discipline of a child: the more effectively parents punish early on, the less they will have to punish later.
- A garden that's virtually weed free is a happier, healthier garden. Its flowers will bloom more vibrantly. Its vegetables will be more nutritious. And so it is with well-disciplined kids: they are happier, healthier, they bloom more vibrantly, and my analogy breaks down at that point because I can't figure out how a well-behaved child is like a broccoli floret. But you get my point.

Before going any further, it needs to be said that effective punishment can only be done out of love. A child who is not completely secure in the knowledge and feeling that his parents love him without reservation will not accept their punishment. You do not need to worry about this though, because the only parents who take the time to read parenting books are parents who love their children without reservation. Now that that's been taken care of . . .

While punishment is regrettably necessary at times, it is not the only means of skinning the cat of bad behavior. Sometimes, it is better to confuse the misbehaving child, to mess with his mind, than to simply punish him.

This is nothing new. Your great-grandmother called it "reverse psychology." My good friend and fellow heretic-psychologist Kevin Leman, the author of *Have a New Kid by Friday!* (a recipient of the coveted Rosemond Seal of Approval) tells the story of a mom who came to him for advice concerning her seven-year-old son.[2] He wouldn't eat the food she fixed for dinner. Kevin asked for an example, and the mother cited spaghetti, to which Kevin simply told the mom to fix spaghetti that evening but not to set a place at the table for her son. Don't even call him to dinner, he instructed.

"When your son wanders into the dining room and asks why no place is set for him," Kevin said, "just point out to him that you're having spaghetti, and he doesn't like it, so you didn't include him in the meal."

The next day, the mother called Kevin and reported that when her son discovered he'd been excluded from the evening meal, he promptly went over to the stove, smelled the spaghetti sauce, and said, "But Mom, I like *this* spaghetti."

Imagine that! Spaghetti anorexia cured in one mealtime!

Here's another fact of living with children: they *like* to misbehave. The reasons:

- They think it's funny.
- They take perverse satisfaction out of upsetting adults.
- Sometimes they get what they want when they misbehave.
- Rebelling against authority gives them a sense of power.
- They often get a lot of attention when they misbehave.
- They discover that they can control certain people and situations by misbehaving.

For all those reasons, misbehavior is addictive, which means it is in a child's best interest that parents do all they can to make sure this particular addiction never takes hold, or if it already has, to cure it as quickly as possible. Paradoxically, children like it when adults help them not to misbehave.

"Now, just you hold on there a darn minute, Rosemond," someone is saying. "You're not making any sense at all! How could children like to misbehave, yet also like it when adults make them stop misbehaving?"

Because children don't know they like behaving properly until adults make them stop misbehaving, at which point they have an awakening of sorts. They realize they really *don't* like misbehaving; they really *don't* like being the center of attention; they really *don't* like entering into power struggles with adults, much less winning them; they really *don't* like getting their way when they really shouldn't. It's at that point that children begin to realize they are happier, more relaxed, more creative, and even smarter (and more like broccoli) when they do what adults expect and tell them to do.

Parenting Axiom Three

The most obedient children are also the happiest children.
(This is also true of adults, by the way.)

That is exactly what the best research into parenting style outcomes has discovered. But common sense will tell you the same thing. Think of some very disobedient children that you know. Do they seem like happy campers to you? No, they don't. They are tense, driven, uptight, angry, rebellious, and petulant. That does not describe someone who is happy.

Now think of some relaxed, happy children that you know. Without exception, they are calmly obedient, aren't they? And just to put a myth to bed, they don't act like they're obeying because they're terrified of what their parents will do if they don't obey, do they? No, they don't. They just obey because they have come to realize, intuitively (children can't articulate these concepts), that *obedience is the ticket to a happy childhood.* Freedom is not the ticket (although obedient children tend to enjoy lots of freedom); money is not the ticket; having a lot of toys is not the ticket; a brand-new bicycle or the coolest and most expensive skateboard is not the ticket; a trip to Dizzy World is not the ticket. Obedience is the ticket! The wonderful thing is that not all parents can afford to give their children new bicycles or trips to Dizzy World, but obedience is free! It costs nothing! And so *every* parent—including you!—can afford to give the gift of obedience to his or her child.

Parenting Axiom Four

Because it is a parent's job to maximize a child's happiness, it is also a parent's job to discipline the child properly so that the child becomes happily obedient.

DOGS AND CHILDREN ARE HORSES OF TWO DIFFERENT COLORS

A dog trainer once told me he thought disciplining a child was really no different than training a dog. I let the remark pass, but the gentleman was wrong. Unlike children, dogs aren't bad. Dogs aren't good either. They are simply dogs. If you teach a dog to walk by your side at the command to heel, it will forever walk at your side when you say, "Heel." Their primary desire is to please their owners. While some dogs can be trained more easily than others, there is no equivalent in the behavior of a dog to a child's "You can't tell me what to do!"

Furthermore, teaching a six-month-old dog to heel will only take a couple of hours, at most. Teaching your three-year-old child to walk by your side will require numerous sessions over several months, and just when you think you have succeeded, your child suddenly decides he doesn't want to obey. He wants to see what's in the next aisle. When you tell him to stop and come back, he ignores you, or worse, he laughs and starts running away. When you finally restore "control" and tell him to hold your hand, he refuses. No, disciplining a child is not remotely similar to training a dog.

But today's parents think it is. The fellow in the dog-training anecdote speaks for a parenting culture that was seduced in the 1960s by the notion that the simple principles of behavior modification work as well on human beings as they do on dogs. In reality, behavior modification *appears* to work on a human subject only when the human *consents* to it. Put another way: a dog lacks the intellectual and emotional acumen needed to mount resistance to a properly wrought behavior modification strategy, but a human being does not—and yes, I am including children as young as two in this truism. Let me remind you that the toddler's battle cry is "You're not the boss of me!" and the teen's is "I don't care what you do to me!" There are no equivalents to these audacities in the behavior of a well-trained dog. A well-trained dog does not growl menacingly at its trainer when told to lie down. It lies down.

Because of behavior modification propaganda, American parents believe that the right consequences, rightly delivered, will produce the right behavior. While that's true with a dog, it's not necessarily true with a human being. With a child, consequences that are appropriate, right, and proper may or may not produce the right behavior. Most children learn their lessons the hard way, and the more important the lesson, the more likely it is that a child will learn it the hard way. Furthermore, as anyone who has raised more than one child to adulthood will testify, it certainly appears that every child comes into the world destined to have incredible difficulty learning at least one particularly pain-filled lesson.

But wait! There's yet another difference between dogs and children: reward and punishment work reliably with dogs. Properly reward what you want the dog to do, and the dog does it. Properly punish what you do not want the dog to do, and the dog stops doing it. But reward and punishment do *not* work reliably with children—or human beings in general, for that matter. Reward what you want a child to do and he may or may not do it, or he may do it for a while and then decide he's had enough of that particular reward and stop doing it. Punish what you want a child to stop doing and the child may keep right on doing it just to prove that there is no authority in his life greater than his own. Parents who do not accept that the discipline of a dog and the discipline of a child are two entirely different propositions are in for a lot of frustration.

Parenting Axiom Five

When a child does the wrong thing and his parents do the right thing,
it is entirely possible that the child will keep on doing the wrong thing
no matter how consistently his parents do the right thing.

Don't get me wrong. Despite the fact that behavior modification does not work with children, it is vital that parents do all they can to teach their kids that bad behavior results in undesirable consequences. It is equally vital that parents understand that, just because their children know they'll be punished for bad behavior does not mean they will not behave badly at times.

With children, proper consequences deliver information. In effect, a punitive consequence (assuming it's appropriate to the situation) conveys this message to a child:

"What you are now experiencing [the consequence] is a scaled-down example of what will likely happen to you if you behave that way as an adult in the real world."

The hope is that your child will be persuaded never to behave in said fashion again—that he will *learn the lesson*. But as I said, some children are more easily persuaded than others. My point: whereas a proper and properly delivered consequence will change the behavior of a dog, a proper and properly delivered consequence simply causes a child to *think*. Hopefully, the child's thinking will result in his deciding to forever abandon the misbehavior in question. But it may not, and if it doesn't, that doesn't mean that the consequence was improper or improperly delivered.

But do not despair, because even when consequences do not have any effect, it is still possible to help a child learn his lessons. Some cakes rise quickly; some slowly.

IT WASN'T BROKE, BUT THEY TRIED TO FIX IT ANYWAY (AND BROKE IT)

I endured graduate school in psychology in the early 1970s. This was psychology's romantic period, during which I was taught that children were good by nature. It followed that a child could be persuaded not to misbehave by doing something as simple as having him sit in a chair for a few minutes when he did. Time-out, as this method is called, was promoted as the be-all, end-all of discipline. During my tenure in private practice, I eventually came to the belated conclusion that the stubborn nature of a child requires discipline that is powerfully persuasive, which time-out is not. Time-out works, I concluded, with children who are already well behaved, in which case it is nothing more than a low-key reminder of expectations. But with a persistently disobedient, disrespectful, or disruptive child, using time-out is akin to trying to fend off a charging elephant with a flyswatter.

At the time, given the general infatuation with time-out, the only other disciplinary alternatives were fairly traditional ones, like spanking, that had fallen into disrepute. In fact, any discipline that smacked of how pre-1960s parents (ergo, supposedly unenlightened parents) might have responded to misbehavior was eschewed and characterized as abusive. When I suggested in a newspaper column in the early 1980s that misbehaving children be sent to their rooms and put to bed early, a number of therapists complained that children so punished stood great likelihood of developing phobias concerning their rooms and perhaps even nightmares. Nonetheless, parents who followed my advice reported positive results, and as far as I can tell, not one child punished using this method developed phobias or nightmares. I began to realize that the more outrageous my recommendations were in the eyes of most of my fellow mental health professionals, the better the results parents reported. As a child's behavior improved, so did his overall attitude, and the emotional atmosphere of the family improved as well. Parents argued less, siblings squabbled less, and everyone communicated better. Who could take issue with that?

Being the punctilious fellow that I am, I began organizing my methods into systems and later into a workshop that, after several trial titles, became "The Well-Behaved Child: Discipline That Really Works!" Over the past several years, numerous parents have helped me further expand and refine my approach, which is not "my" approach at all, really, but a fine-tuning of a very traditional approach to discipline.

That S-Word Thing

Before I go any further, I need to make one thing perfectly clear: a traditional approach to discipline was not and is not synonymous with spanking. Yes, traditional discipline usually included the option of spanking, but it was an option utilized rarely by most pre-1960s parents. Many, if not most, people my age will tell you that they can count on one hand the number of times they were spanked as kids. I believe spanking can be a reasonable response to certain outrageous misbehaviors, if you follow these common-sense guidelines for why and when and how to spank.

- Reserve spanking for *big offenses*.
- Do not use spanking as a primary form of discipline. In other words, spank only occasionally, when *big offenses* occur. The more often you spank, the less effective any given spanking will be.
- If you are spanking for a *big offense*, and the misbehavior does not stop, then stop spanking for it. Obviously, the spankings aren't working. Instead, use one of the methods I describe in chapter 3.
- Before administering a spanking, explain to your child why you are spanking. Don't lecture, but let your child know that you've decided to spank in order to help him remember not to do whatever he did again. This is another way of saying don't spank in anger. But make sure you spank with determination.

- Use your bare hand. Contrary to the myth, using your hand is not confusing to a child. Besides, if you use your hand, you'll know when you have caused sufficient pain. Ergo, you'll know when to stop. That's not the case if you use an object like a paddle.
- After a spanking, sit with your child until he has calmed down. Tell him you love him and that your love for him is why you simply will not let him get away with misbehavior.

Oh, by the way, the notion that spanking teaches children that it's okay to hit other people is pure, unmitigated malarkey. Research done by eminent and ethical social scientists finds that children who are occasionally (the operative word) spanked score higher on measures of social and emotional adjustment than children who are never spanked. One study even found that children who have never been spanked are *more* aggressive than kids who have experienced spanking's purgative powers.

Rewards, or How to Grow a Manipulative Child

Adele Faber and other new-fashioned parenting experts believe children can be reasoned with. That's a very romantic notion, and I've "been there, done that." Early in my career as a psychologist, I believed likewise, which is one of the reasons my wife, Willie, and I experienced so much psychic pain during our early parenting years. Because I believed children could be reasoned with, and I persuaded Willie to go along with that and other cockamamy ideas, our children ran the Rosemond family for a good number of years.

When I finally recovered from the narcotic effects of my graduate school indoctrination, I realized, among many other things, that punishing bad behavior made perfect sense. First, punishment assigns complete responsibility for the problem to the person who produced the problem. No other response to misbehavior accomplishes this. Second, by associating discomfort or inconvenience with misbehavior, punishment makes it less likely that the problem will rear its ugly head ever again.

The babblemeisters of postmodern psychological parenting demonized the sort of punitive approach to behavior problems I advocate. But then, anything that bore some resemblance to the "old" way of raising children was fair game to them. I unabashedly admit that most of my tactics are old-fashioned, but I happen to believe that, for the most part, the old-fashioned parenting point of view and the methods employed by parents of the pre–psychological parenting age (1950s and before) are far more functional and effective than the point of view and methods that have replaced them. Reward-based discipline strategies are one of the nouveau methods in question, and as is the case with most of what the professional babblemeisters recommend, giving rewards to a misbehaving child (when he behaves) doesn't work. In fact, rewards given under those circumstances are very likely to backfire.

The primary problem with reward-based strategies is that they bear little, if any, relationship to the way the world actually works. To illustrate, let's suppose your job performance is consistently below par. You come in late, fail to fill your quota or turn in reports on time, and often leave early. Your supervisor counsels you concerning these problems, but his words and warnings fall on deaf ears. One day, he posts a chart above your desk and announces, "Every day you come to work on time, turn in your reports, fill your quotas, and stay the full eight hours, I'll glue a star in one of the fifty blocks on this chart. When you've earned fifty stars, we're going to reward you with a new car, any car you want!"

Fat chance, eh? But for the purposes of this discussion, let's pretend your supervisor does exactly that. Would you get your act in gear and begin earning stars for cars? Sure you would! And once you were behind the wheel of your new Lasagnaginni TurboMax NovaSport 4000, you'd slowly but surely begin reverting to your old, irresponsible ways at work. You'd even take a certain pleasure in your supervisor's mounting exasperation, knowing that the more exasperated he becomes, the more likely he is to make you an even better offer than the first one. Earning the new car didn't, therefore, make you a better employee. Quite the contrary, it taught you how to manipulate your boss.

Likewise, reward-based discipline strategies teach children how to manipulate their parents. They teach children that misbehavior and underachievement are the tickets to getting special privileges. It doesn't take them long to realize—at an intuitive level—that adults don't make these generous offers to well-behaved, highly motivated children. Conclusion: misbehavior pays.

Reward-based plans carry a built-in time bomb I call the Saturation Principle.

The Saturation Principle

Sooner or later, any child will reach a saturation point with any reward, at which point the reward will cease to be motivating.

A certain reward might have been initially enticing enough to leverage improved behavior or performance in a child, but when saturation occurs—when, in other words, the child has "had his fill" of the reward—his interest in the reward will decline along with his behavior or performance. At this point, in order to pump up the child's performance again, his parents must make him another offer, more interesting than the first. Under the circumstances, therefore, the parents are taking responsibility for maintaining the child's performance at adequate levels. As such, the child cannot begin to appreciate the intrinsic value of improving himself.

Back to the hypothetical story of you, the misbehaving employee. After counseling (the obligatory attempt to reason with you) has failed to produce lasting change in your behavior, your supervisor is going to take you aside and inform you that unless your work performance shows immediate improvement, and continues to do so, he's going to fire you. In other words, he's going to invoke what I call the Godfather Principle (see chapter 2): he's going to make you an offer you can't refuse—not, at least, if you have any sense.

The motivation to maintain one's standard of living is universal. Adults measure their standards of living in terms of purchasing power.

Children measure their standards of living in terms of freedom and privilege. So, to motivate a child to change his or her behavior, all you need to do is reduce the child's standard of living.

Another reason rewards don't work—or only work for a short time and then stop working—is because they are not essential elements of a child's day-to-day standard of living. They are add-ons, extras. As such, they constitute offers children *can* refuse. Small reductions of privilege fall into the same category. Taking a child's television privileges away for a day means nothing to the child. He will simply put the time he would have spent watching television into some other pursuit and be perfectly content in the process. If you want misbehavior to stop, you have to make an impression.

To make a proper impression on a misbehaving child, you first need to understand discipline's foundational principles. That's where we're going next. Step right this way.

CHAPTER TWO

The Seven Fundamentals of Effective Discipline

Today's parents believe that for any behavior problem, there is a right method or technique that will solve it. Indeed, it's important that you select your approach to a behavior problem strategically, with an eye to your child's age, the severity and duration of the problem, and so on. But the essence of successful discipline is not a collection of right methods but rather a right *point of view*. Without the right point of view, no method will work for long. With the right point of view, just about any strategically chosen method will work and keep right on working. The purpose of this chapter is to help you acquire that right point of view. I'm not going to say anything new. In essence, I'm going to describe the point of view that was held by most parents—the overwhelming number, in fact—prior to the psychological-parenting revolution that swept America in the 1960s and early 1970s. Your great-grandmother, maybe even your grandmother, knew this stuff. They knew it *intuitively* because they were in touch with common sense. Since the 1960s, a big wet blanket of psychobabble has smothered parenting common sense in America. My aim in this chapter is to help you do away with the big wet blanket so your common sense can breathe again.

To begin the liberation of your common sense, I'm going to set up a hypothetical situation and then ask you a question.

I ask the superintendent of a large school system if I can observe, in his or her classroom, the teacher in the system who consistently has the fewest discipline problems of any teacher in the system, regardless of the students she is assigned. The superintendent directs me to the classroom of fifth-grade teacher Fredrika Schmock. I sit in on Ms. Schmock's class for several days, paying particular attention to the manner in which she disciplines. Am I watching a teacher who disciplines her students by manipulating reward and punishment? In other words, is Ms. Schmock using behavior modification to create a disciplined classroom?

The answer, of course, is no. Ms. Schmock is not disciplining her students by using "classroom behavior strategies" based on a behavior modification paradigm. She is disciplining her students by *presenting* herself to them in a certain way. If I were to use one word to describe the Ms. (and Mr.) Schmocks of the world, it would be *charismatic.* Not in the religious sense of the term, mind you, but in the sense of being poised, self-assured, calm, confident, cool under fire, compelling, and interesting. Her students are well behaved (even ones who are not well behaved with other teachers) because she acts like she knows what she is doing. Furthermore, they realize that she has their best interests at heart. She is not all about behavior modification; she is all about Leadership, with a capital *L.* In everything she does—from the way she walks into the classroom to the way she writes on the blackboard to the way she talks to her class—she radiates Authority, with a capital *A.* In her classroom, she is clearly Alpha—the Big Dog. She is where it's at. She's the epitome of cool. Interestingly enough, she is liked by her students, but she is not trying to be liked.

The parents of Ms. Schmock's students could learn a lot from her, beginning with how to talk so children will pay attention and do what they are expected to do.

ALPHA SPEECH

With rare exception, today's parents think discipline is all about correcting misbehavior by manipulating reward and punishment. They believe, in short, in behavior modification.

I talked some about the fallacy of behavior modification in chapter 1, but a brief review is in order.

Behavior modification—the popular name for operant conditioning—posits that the same principles that govern the behavior of dogs, rats, and other animals also govern the behavior of human beings. Harvard psychologist Burrhus Frederick Skinner (1904–1990) was the first to propose that operant conditioning methods would work equally well on humans and animals. Even though he never succeeded at proving his contention, Skinner's mechanistic philosophy became one of the mainstays of postmodern psychological parenting. The truth, however, is that behavior modification does *not* work on human beings.[1] When it appears to work, it only does so because the human subjects in question decide it is in their best interest to cooperate. In other words, whether or not behavior modification appears to work on a human being is a matter of that human being's *choosing*, which is to say, it is a matter of free will.

Consequences hold sway over the behavior of animals, but they do not hold sway over the behavior of humans. A dog, for example, does not possess the ability—the strength of will—to resist the persuasive effect of a consequence. For this reason, if a dog trainer uses the right combination of rewards and punishments, he will obtain the behavior he wants from the dog. If he fails to obtain the desired behavior, it is proper to conclude that he did not manipulate consequences properly. But this same reasoning does not apply when the subject is a human being—for our purposes, a child.

Unlike a dog, a child possesses the strength of will to resist the persuasive power of a consequence—to deny that a consequence, no matter how powerful, has any power in his life. This is why so many children are called "strong willed." They persist in misbehavior no matter what.

Their parents are often heard saying they've tried everything, but nothing works. By "everything," they mean every behavior modification strategy they could think of or find in a book or magazine.

These very strong-willed children don't have biochemical imbalances, abnormalities in the brains, or any other such pseudoscientific nonsense.[2] They just have an overabundance of human nature. They are rebels without a cause. Humans, unlike dogs, are rebellious by nature. Some children express this very outwardly and some express it quietly, cleverly. A simple way of putting this is that whereas your dog wants it *your* way, your child wants it *his* way. But so do you.

We are all strong willed, but most adults accept that we can't always have our own way (and when we do get our way, we learn to do so without calling lots of attention to ourselves). But some folks just keep trying to bash their way through life. They started down this road as toddlers, and toddlers they remain. You know such people. We all do.

It's important that I clarify something here. I've said that behavior modification is all about the manipulation of consequences, and behavior modification does not work on human beings. I am *not* saying, however, that when a child misbehaves, consequences are pointless or a waste of time and energy. I'm simply saying that one does not accomplish the successful discipline of a child by manipulating consequences. Nonetheless, it is important that parents do all they can to help children learn that in the real world misbehavior results in negative outcomes. This is done by exposing children to what I call the Backatcha Principle: *when you do something bad, something bad will happen to you, sooner or later.*

What parents have to accept, however, is that some children learn the Backatcha Principle readily and some stubbornly refuse to accept that it applies to them. Your job, therefore, is not to make sure your children *learn* the Backatcha Principle. That's out of your control. Your job is to *teach* it as well as you can. But remember, you're working with a human being here, not a dog. No matter how well you teach the Backatcha Principle, you cannot guarantee that your child will learn it. By delivering negative consequences (punishing) when a child misbehaves, you are simply hoping the child will wake up and "get it." And let's face it: some kids get it more quickly than others, just like some kids catch on to math more quickly than others. Ah, but there are ways of helping kids get it more quickly, ways I will discuss later, but soon enough.

Making a Disciple of Your Child

We've established that the proper discipline of a child is *not* accomplished simply through the delivery of proper consequences, although consequences are absolutely necessary. The answer to the question "How, then, is the proper discipline of a child accomplished?" requires that we focus on the root of the word *discipline*, which is *disciple*. The literal meaning of *discipline* is the process by which you transform your child into a disciple. A disciple is someone who subscribes willingly to the authority of his or her teacher, who believes that the teacher speaks the truth, and that by following the teacher, his or her life will be greatly improved.

A child-disciple, then, is defined by four qualities:

1. He knows he can rely on his parents (trust).
2. He looks up to his parents (respect).
3. He follows their lead (obedience).
4. He subscribes to their values (loyalty).

This transformation—turning the "terrible" toddler into a prosocial human being—is accomplished by providing the child proper *leadership*, one of the two ingredients in truly effective parenting, the other being unconditional love.[3]

This is probably a new concept to you. If you're like most parents, you've never associated parenting with leadership. You are probably asking yourself, *What does parent-leadership look like?* Actually, you already know the answer to that question because at some time in your life you have either provided effective leadership to a person or group of people or you have been the recipient of it, and leadership is leadership. The same principles that govern leadership in the military or a corporation also govern the leadership of children in the home.

Are effective leaders defined in terms of how well they manipulate reward and punishment? Is effective leadership a matter of delivering consequences properly? Of course not. Effective leaders are defined primarily in terms of their communication skills. They are masters of inspiring, authoritative speech—what I call Alpha Speech. When they talk, no one doubts that they know what they're talking about. Effective leaders are decisive, which reflects the confidence they possess in their vision, their command of the proverbial big picture. Effective leaders say what they mean and mean what they say. As such, they can be relied upon. They also tend not to give explanations for the decisions they make, and when they do express their rationale, they do so concisely. They know that when someone in a position of authority explains the reason behind an executive decision, he runs the risk of conveying that he's not quite sure of himself. In other words, explanations are the stock-in-trade of indecisive people, and indecisiveness does not make for good leadership. The greatest leader of all time, Jesus, said as much when He exhorted His disciples during the Sermon on the Mount: "Let your 'Yes' be 'Yes,' and your 'No,' 'No'" (Matthew 5:37 NKJV).

Do you, by and large, use Alpha Speech in your communication with your children? Do you talk authoritatively? Are you decisive? Do you stand by your decisions? Do you avoid explanations?

When it comes to conveying instructions and expectations to children, most of today's parents use more words than are necessary. Furthermore, they often tack the question "Okay?" onto the end of what they *think* are instructions to their children, as in "I need to use this room to talk to a friend of mine who's coming over in a few minutes, and I'd like to have a neat area for us to meet in; so how about let's get these toys picked up now, okay?" You may recognize yourself in that example. That is about as far from Alpha Speech as one can get.

In that same situation, Alpha Speech sounds like this: "It's time for you to pick up these toys. I'll be back in a few minutes to see that it's done." At that point, Alpha Parent walks casually out of the room, implying, *I know you're going to obey me.* Note the conciseness of that instruction. It's an example of what old-fashioned parents, fifty-plus years ago, referred to as "short and sweet." Here are two important facts:

1. The fewer words a parent uses, the more authoritative the parent sounds.
2. The fewer words a parent uses, the more clear the instruction.

Putting those two facts together:

The "Short and Sweet" Principle

The fewer words a parent uses when giving instructions or
conveying expectations, the more likely it is that the child will obey.

The verbose mother in the previous example does nothing but waste a lot of words. Her explanation—that she wanted the toys picked up because a friend was coming over and she wants the room to be neat for their meeting —is completely unnecessary. The explanation clutters up her message and conveys that she is trying to persuade instead of give an instruction. Mom need not, and should not, justify why she wants her child to pick up his toys. The fact that she wants it done is reason enough. Furthermore, the explanation that she has a friend coming over and they need that room invites push back, as in an argument. I'll get to that momentarily.

> **Great News!**
>
> An adult does not need to justify him- or herself to a child. That means you! *You* do not need to justify any decision you make to your child! Isn't that great news?

The Four Most Powerful Words in Parenting

All of this brings me to four of the most powerful words you can master: "Because I said so." Mainstream parenting pundits have told two generations of parents that those four words squash a child's natural curiosity, insult a child's intelligence, disrespect a child, teach a child that might makes right, and so on. That is nothing but pure, refined blah-blah-blah. Fifty-plus years ago, children heard those four words (or variations on them) nearly every time they challenged their parents' authority by asking "Why?" or "Why not?" And make no mistake about it, those are challenges to authority; they are not legitimate questions. When your child asks one of those "questions," he is trying to make you justify yourself. And if you fall into that clever trap, you are opening the door to argument.

If that doesn't sit well with you, consider the fact that children only whine "Why?" or "Why not?" when they *don't* like decisions their parents have made. Will your child shrug his shoulders defiantly and whine "Why?" if you say, "We're going to Disney World tomorrow!"? No, he will not. Will he demand to know "Why not?" if you tell him you're *not* serving poached rutabaga with pureed turnipseed sauce for dinner? Not a chance. Those facts disqualify "Why?" and "Why not?" as legitimate questions (and, of course, I'm not referring to the use of "Why?" and "Why not?" when a child requests information that has nothing to do with instructions from you, as in a child who asks "Why?" in response to "Planets don't twinkle; stars do") and expose them for what they are: invitations to do battle. Children know that if they can lure their parents into argument, they stand a chance, however slim, of getting their way. And a slim chance is better than no chance at all.

Now think on this: has your child ever—after you gave the best, most eloquent explanation you could think of for "Why?" or "Why not?" (the rebellious forms)—paused for thought and said, "Thanks, Mom and Dad, for helping me understand why I should eat this poached rutabaga, and believe me, I really appreciate your concern for my overall health"? No way. Immediately following an explanation, your child comes back with a counterpoint or negotiation: "How about if I eat one more bite of biscuit instead?" or "But I don't *like* rutabaga!" And the argument escalates from there.

If you answer your child's "Why?" or "Why not?" with anything other than "Because I say so" (or an equally short and sweet variation on that simple theme),[4] you are stepping right into quicksand. In our opening story, the child whose mother has just asked him to pick up his toys before her guest arrives can come back with, "But you can use another room!" or "I was here first!" Again—and I can't stress it enough—giving reasons opens the door to argument, and an adult who enters into argument with a child has already lost because *effective leaders do not argue with the people they lead, ever*. The minute you enter into an argument with your child, you have stripped yourself of authority.

"Because I said so" is nothing more than a statement of leadership. It says, "As the adult here and as your parent, I don't need to, nor will I, justify myself to you. You will do what I tell you to do because I told you to do it. Period." But it says all that in four words. Remember, authority figures do not use twenty words when four will do. They let their "yes" be "yes" and their "no" be "no."

When you become truly adept at using "Because I said so," you will find yourself using it less and less. Your child will stop challenging you with "Why?" and "Why not?" because he will know the answer. "Because I said so" will also greatly simplify your child's life. It will release him from the obsessive need to test your authority. In the final analysis, this makes for a much more relaxed parent-child relationship.

My grandson Jack, when he was about seven, came to visit our house one afternoon, and while he was there he asked me for something. I said no. He shrugged his body in frustration and blurted, "Why not?" with no small degree of insolence.

I calmly looked at him for a few seconds and then said, "Jack, you've known me now for seven years. You've been around me a lot, and you've heard me answer that same question before, many times. What's the answer?"

His face fell, and he mumbled, "Because you say so."

And that was that. Jack is fourteen now (and truly the most well-mannered and respectful young teenager I've ever known), and he often calls me when I'm in town just wanting to "hang out" with Grandpa. He and I have a wonderful relationship in large part because he knows where I stand. He also knows that when I take a stand, I cannot be moved.

He may not always like it that Grandpa is so "inflexible," but it certainty relieves him of the need to waste lots of energy challenging my authority. Our relationship is more relaxed, and therefore more fun, because he (and his brothers and cousins) know exactly what to expect from me (and their grandmother, Willie, as well).

In a sense, this is about being a "mean" parent, but I'm not talking about being cruel, hateful, spiteful, or sadistic. I'm talking about saying what you *mean* and *mean*ing what you say. In that light, one of the greatest compliments your child can give you is to tell you that you are "mean." He won't intend it as such, of course, but it's a compliment nonetheless. Therefore, anytime your child accuses you of being mean, your proper response is, "That's right, and thank you!"

Acting Like a Leader

We've established that your child will be successfully disciplined only if you assume your rightful authority in your child's life and act like a leader, which is to say your actions convey four attributes:

1. You act like you know what you're doing. (You are decisive.)
2. You act like you know where you're going. (You have a vision that guides your decisions.)
3. You act like you know what you want your child to do. (You are assertively direct; you don't beat around the bush when it comes to giving instructions.)
4. You act like you know your child is going to obey and/or live up to your expectations. (You are positive, optimistic, self-assured, and inspiring; you bring out the best in people.)

Take note of the fact that in each case, I said the parent is *acting*. In other words, not only do you know what you're doing, but you are also *acting* like you know what you're doing. You're conveying—in your body language, tone of voice, and facial expression—that you are supremely confident in the decisions you're making and the direction you're taking.

It's the difference between saying, "I want you to pick up these toys now" with a worried expression and saying it with a self-assured expression.

To help yourself get with the new parenting program you've undertaken, make a poster of your new parenting creed and magnetize it to your refrigerator or tack it to your kitchen bulletin board. If your children ask what it means, just say, "It means there's a new sheriff in town."

My Parenting Creed

I know what I'm doing.
I know where I'm going.
I know what I want.
I know I'm going to get it.

Leaders project these four qualities by successfully employing Alpha Speech, which is not simply a matter of the words that come out of one's mouth, but also one's tone of voice, facial expression, and body language. The most effective leaders are casual, comfortable in their authority, and matter-of-fact. Does that describe the majority of today's parents? Absolutely not! Stressed, uncomfortable in their authority, and vague would be more like it. If you recognize yourself here, take heart, because you can remedy your Leadership Deficiency Disorder fairly easily by learning how to speak to your child using Alpha Speech. In fact, you're going to quickly discover that using Alpha Speech requires a lot less effort than its opposite, Milquetoast Speech.

Caspar Milquetoast was a character created in 1924 by Harold Webster for his long-running comic strip *The Timid Soul*. Milquetoast was the antithesis of assertive. He was shy, uncertain, indecisive, and let other people walk all over him. Most of today's parents talk to their children using Milquetoast Speech, speech that's timid and unassertive. Consequently, many children are walking all over their parents.

The previous example of the mother asking her child to pick up his toys is Milquetoast Speech. Here it is again: "I need to use this room to talk to a friend of mine who's coming over in a few minutes, and I'd like to have a neat area for us to meet in; so how about let's get these toys picked up now, okay?" What does that mean? If it's not *okay* with her child, he doesn't have to do it?

I once challenged parents, through my syndicated newspaper column, to count the number of times they tacked ". . . okay?" onto the end of a supposed instruction to their kids. One mother reported that she had used ". . . okay?" nearly fifty times in one day, with only one child! She confessed that even though she was trying not to use it, it would slip out automatically. Yes, bad habits are hard to break, but they can be broken. Here's how: before giving an instruction to your child, ask yourself: "What do I want my child to do, and how can I phrase it in the most authoritative way possible, using the least number of words?" Practice asking yourself that question; then practice using Alpha Speech. Within weeks you're going to find it beginning to come very naturally. To get you started, here are several contrasts between Alpha Speech and Milquetoast Speech:

Milquetoast (the old you): "We've been at the park long enough, don't you think? How about let's go home now, okay?" (This parent has invited resistance and defiance.)

Alpha (the new you!): "We've been here long enough. It's time to leave. What's that? You don't want to go? I understand that you're having fun, but we're going nonetheless."

Milquetoast: "I don't think it's a good idea for you to be out so late with those boys. I've heard some things about them that make me uncomfortable, and I'm just concerned that you might get in a problem situation with them." (This parent has invited an argument and will almost certainly get one.)

Alpha: "Why can't you stay out late with your friends? Listen carefully: because I said so."

Milquetoast: "I'd really appreciate it if you'd rake the lawn today. It would be great if you could get it done before noon. Do you think that's possible?" (Child begins complaining.)

Alpha: "Today is the day you're going to rake the lawn. It needs to be done before noon." (Child may begin complaining, but since Alpha Parent has already left the room, the child has no audience.)

Milquetoast: "You might want to think about beginning to put these things away so that I can set the table for supper, okay?" (Child acts like she hasn't heard a thing.)

Alpha: "It's time to put those things away and set the table for me."

You're about to make your life—and your child's—a whole lot easier!

Before We Move On

It's important to understand that leadership can be effective without being ethical. Some very bad guys have been effective leaders. (Think Hitler, Stalin, and Castro.) The difference between ethical and unethical leaders is that ethical leaders act primarily not for their *own* benefit but for the benefit of others. They expect the best of people, they try to bring out the best in people, and they help people do their best.

This is what parenting is all about: providing leadership to children so that they become the best people they are capable of becoming. It starts with the L-words *love* and *leadership*, and it culminates with your children leaving home and showing you what a good job you did.

NIPPING IT IN THE BUD

Today's parenting pundits are fond of giving you two tidbits of equally bad, and I mean *really bad*, advice: "Don't sweat the small stuff" and

"Choose your battles carefully." Essentially, they mean the same thing. Those tired clichés may apply to some misbehavior, but small misbehaviors often carry the potential of quickly growing into *huge* problems. That's why your great-grandmother advised her children, when they became parents, to "nip it in the bud"—to respond firmly and forcefully when a certain misbehavior first rears its potentially ugly head.

Children who are generally well behaved sometimes experiment with misbehavior just to see what sort of reaction they'll get. Sometimes, a child will watch another child misbehave—he blatantly ignores an instruction from his parents, for example—and asks himself, *I wonder what my parents would do if I ignored them?* When the next opportunity presents itself, he ignores them. If his parents respond ineffectively to this little test, the child is likely to ignore them again at the next possible opportunity. If that next experiment "succeeds," he will ignore them again, and again, and again. Pretty soon, the parents have a major problem on their hands. That's an example of how small stuff can develop into *huge* stuff, and quickly.

In most cases, misbehavior should be nipped in the bud. Be consistently intolerant of misbehavior, but don't get all bent out of shape over it. Be calmly purposeful in your intolerance. Let your children know, right off the bat, that you will accept nothing less than proper behavior at all times in all circumstances. If you don't demonstrate consistent, calm intolerance of misbehavior, you invite little experiments like the one I just described.

The "Nipping" Principle

Don't sweat it; *get* it!

Nipping misbehavior in the bud requires that you observe three guidelines:

1. **Tell 'em once!** Don't insult your child's intelligence by repeating instructions or reminding him of the same rule (i.e. "When you finish your shower, hang up your towels") over and over again.

2. **Do what you can, when you can.** Contrary to what you may have heard, you don't have to punish misbehavior as soon as it occurs. Language-based memory begins to form around the third birthday; so if your child is three or older, you can delay the delivery of a consequence for a period of time equivalent to the child's memory span (i.e., twenty-four hours for a three-year-old; several days for a five-year-old; a week for a nine-year-old). When you are delaying consequences, you are only required to clearly describe the precipitating misbehavior: exactly what happened, when, and where. Under the circumstances, your child *will* make the connection.

3. **The punishment should never fit the crime.** This is the essence of "nipping." If, in your opinion, a certain misbehavior merits a rating of 2 (on a scale of 1 to 10), the punishment should be a 7. That prevents the misbehavior from growing from a 2 to a 7.

Let's consider a rather typical example of small misbehavior and see how these guidelines apply. A mother pulls into the parking lot at her local shopping center and turns to her three- and six-year-olds in the backseat. She says, using Alpha Speech, "I need to buy three things at this store. [She knows what she's doing.] I need you to stay right by my side while we're in there." [She knows what she wants!] As she unbuckles their seat belts, she says, "I know you're going to obey me." [She believes she'll get what she wants!] She calmly enters the store, her kids by her side.

Five minutes later, the six-year-old spots a toy in another aisle and takes off. Here's what this mother *doesn't* do. She *doesn't* get bug-eyed and yell, "Didn't I tell you to stay right next to me? Why do you make me repeat myself like this? I'm going to tell you one more time: Stand by me! Now!"

That's the way the Old Sheriff might have reacted, but there's a New Sheriff in town. The New Sheriff simply retrieves the child and says nothing. She gets the rest of the items on her list, calmly, as if it's the most natural thing in the world to do. (The New Sheriff doesn't repeat instructions. She tells her child something *once* and *once* only.) Perhaps her six-year-old says, "I was just looking!" in which case, the New Sheriff says, "You can help me with my list if you'd like," and goes right on shopping. Perhaps her child helps. Perhaps he doesn't. It doesn't make any difference. The offense has already taken place, you see? Her child did not do what he was told, the first time he was told.

Once the shopping is finished, the New Sheriff does what she can, when she can. Perhaps she can do something right away. When they're buckled up again, she might say, "Now that my errands are finished, I'm sorry to tell you that we aren't going to the movies this afternoon as we'd planned. Furthermore, you're going to bed right after supper."

"Why?!" her child asks, in the most distressed, dramatic voice imaginable.

"Because you didn't stay by my side like I told you to. From now on, I'm only going to tell you something once; furthermore, when I tell you to do something, I expect you to do it."

"But I was just looking for a minute!" the child exclaims.

"Listen carefully," the New Sheriff says. "We're not going to the movies this afternoon, and you're going to bed right after supper." At that point, she puts the car in gear and heads home, leaving her son to, as my grandmother would have put it, "stew in his own juices."

Note that the New Sheriff, unlike the Old Sheriff, does not engage in an unproductive exchange with her child when he claims he was just looking at something for a minute when he ran away from her. She just drives home.

A reader interrupts: "But John! If I ignore my child at that point, he's just going to cry or badger me to change my mind."

Hold that thought. I'll tell you how to handle that in a moment. First, however, I need to answer the question, "What if the New Sheriff can't punish the child right away? What if they have to go straight to an appointment with the dentist?"

The child in our example is six years old. That means the New Sheriff has at least five days within which to do something about the shopping incident. That evening, at six thirty, as the family is finishing supper, she looks across the table at her son.

"Are you done with your supper?" she asks.

"Yes."

"Then you may be excused. I want you to go upstairs and get ready for bed. Dad and I will be up in a few minutes to help you say your prayers and tuck you in for a good night's sleep."

The child looks confused. He says, "But it's only six thirty."

"That's right," the New Sheriff says. "It's time for bed. And by the way, your bedtime for the next seven days is six thirty."

The child looks alarmed. "Why?" he fusses.

"At eleven o'clock this morning, before we went to the store, I told you to stay right next to me in the store. Instead of obeying, you chose to run away from me and look at toys. Now, go upstairs and get ready for bed."

If the New Sheriff has to wait several days to do something about the shopping incident (the grandparents are visiting, for example), so be it. Three days after it occurred, the child comes running in the house, excited, out of breath.

"Mom!" he exclaims. "Rolando's mom has asked me if I want to go with them to see that new Disney movie! She says she'll pay for my ticket and my popcorn and my drink! Can I go? Please? Can I go?"

The New Sheriff thinks for a moment and then says, "No, sweetie."

"Why?" her child asks, bewildered.

The New Sheriff says, "Three days ago, we went shopping together. I told you I needed you to stay right with me in the store. I gave you the chance to do so on your own, but as soon as I looked away you ran away from me to look at a toy. Because you didn't obey me three days ago, you won't be going to the movies with Rolando and his mother this afternoon."

Then the New Sheriff gets up and walks away, which brings me back to the question asked earlier, "But what if my child follows me, badgering me relentlessly?"

That calls for . . .

The Chair of Wisdom

If you have a child who won't take no for an answer, who follows and badgers and nags and whines and cries and is generally unceasing in his attempts to make you change your "no" to a "yes," you need a designated "Chair of Wisdom."[5]

The designated chair should be comfortable and easily accessible. I recommend an upholstered armchair that is comfortable for relatively long periods of sitting. Whenever your child becomes relentless in her attempts to get you to change your mind, simply say, "I see it's time for the Chair of Wisdom!"

Go straight to the designated chair, sit down, and say to your child, who has been right behind you the whole time, "Now is your chance to try to change my mind. Say everything you can think of. You can cry and scream if you want. I'm just going to sit here for as long as it takes to convince you that my first answer was my final answer. So go ahead."

The overwhelming likelihood is that your child will stand there for a few moments, and then storm away with great drama, perhaps even yelling things like "You're weird!" or "I wish you weren't my mother!" But in the event that your child takes you up on your challenge, just sit and listen to the harangue, nodding your head. Every once in a while, say, "I understand" or, "Yes. If I were your age, I'd feel the same way." Every so often, say, "My answer is still no, but you're doing a great job of expressing yourself."

After your child has had a handful of experiences with just how wise you become when you occupy the Chair of Wisdom, it will become less and less necessary to utilize. In time, all you'll need to say when your child starts badgering is "Do you think we need to go over to the Chair of Wisdom and continue this discussion?" and the badgering will stop.

Yes, a strategy of this sort is bound to be extremely frustrating to a child, to which my sole comment is, "So?" Better the child be frustrated and the parent remain cool than both parent and child wind up furious at one another. Furthermore, there is nothing more lacking in today's parenting than a sense of humor. A child may not like the Chair of Wisdom when she's six, but she'll be laughing uproariously at the memory when she's thirty-six.

THE AGONY AND THE GODFATHER PRINCIPLES

When our now forty-something-year-old son, Eric, was two weeks into the fifth grade, I received a call from his homeroom teacher. She informed me that when she had resolved her grade book earlier that day, she noticed that Eric had not completed even one assignment since the beginning of the school year. A check with his other two teachers revealed that his academic record was "perfect": no completed assignments in any subject area.

"Mind you," she said, almost apologetically, "other than the fact that he's somewhat inattentive, he's not a problem in class. He's very smart and very funny and very popular. He entertains us all, but he's obviously more interested in his social standing than his schoolwork."

I was delighted to hear that Eric's behavior was not a problem, but I was not much interested in his social standing.

"Mrs. Rosemond and I will take care of it, be assured," I said.

"I knew I could count on you," she said. "I'm sure you'll have a very interesting conversation with Eric this evening."

It was interesting, indeed, but I'm equally sure it was not the conversation she had in mind. Willie and I talked, got our game plan in order, and then sat down with Eric. I told him about his teacher's phone call. He just stared at us.

"Here's how we're going to handle this, Eric," I continued. "At present, Mom and I do not ask you questions about or check your homework. That's been your responsibility, and it will continue to be your responsibility. We are not going to begin looking over your shoulder to see if you're doing what you're supposed to be doing in school. So what we're going to do about this is absolutely nothing, for the time being, at least. We're going to simply give you notice that we know about the problem. And we expect you to fix it. Your report card comes out in seven weeks. You think that's enough time to take care of this problem?"

"Yes sir," he answered in a voice that was a bit higher in pitch than usual.

And that was that. Seven weeks went by during which Willie and I did not once ask, "Do you have homework?" or "Have you done your homework?" Nor did we ask to check his work. I simply sent a note to his teachers telling them that the situation was under control at home and to please give Eric the grades he deserved.

His report card came. It did not surprise Willie and me in the least that he received three Ds. We were fairly certain, in fact, that two of them had been gifts. The teachers asked for a conference, so we called and made the appointment.

They told us they were very concerned. Eric was in danger of failing the fifth grade. They were dedicated to not letting that happen. In that regard, they recommended that they send home, every day, a list of his homework, including any work he had failed to finish in class. They wanted us to make sure he did it. Much to their surprise, I told them that it was Eric's responsibility to get through the fifth grade, that we were *not* going to make it our responsibility. Furthermore, if he couldn't handle fifth grade responsibilities, then he obviously wasn't ready to go to the sixth grade, and that was fine with us. We didn't want him in the wrong grade. They sat in stunned silence, obviously not expecting this. I suggested we all get back together in a month's time to see where things stood, to which they agreed.

When we got home, we sat Eric down. "You had seven weeks to solve the problem, kiddo," I began. "You didn't solve it, which means Mom and I have to get involved. I've told you not to get us involved in your responsibilities at school, haven't I?"

"Yes sir," he immediately replied, obviously sensing that something was up.

"Well, you've gotten us involved now. We have an appointment with your teachers in a month. That meeting will begin with us asking how you're doing. All three of your teachers must give the same answer: 'Eric is doing fine; splendidly, in fact. The problem is solved. There's nothing to talk about. End of meeting.'

"If one teacher tells us that you are doing better but still have room for improvement, or if she says anything less than that you have *completely* cleared up this matter, then you'll be in your room for another month."

His eyes widened; his face jutted forward; his mouth fell open. "What?!"

"You'll be in your room for another month."

"What does that mean?!"

"It means you're in your room for a month, Eric. For the next month, unless you are in school, at church, using the bathroom, eating a meal with us, going somewhere with us, or doing a chore around the house, you are in your room. Furthermore, during this month, your bedtime is seven o'clock, lights out, Friday and Saturday nights included. And if at seven o'clock you tell us you still have homework to do, you are going to bed anyway, lights out. During this next month, we are not once going to ask if you have homework or ask to check it or any other such nonsense. Your schoolwork has been, is, and will forever be *your* responsibility."

I ended by saying, "Eric, you have seven years left to live with us, and believe me, we are capable of keeping you in your room for seven years. Your life will still be better than the lives of most of the world's children: you have a nice room. And if you decide to stay in your room for seven years, you can bet that when you turn sixteen, there will be no driver's license because you won't need one. And you can bet that if and when you graduate from high school, there will be no college because we are not sending a child to college who cannot figure out how to get out of his room."

He began pleading. He promised to do better. He said he'd just gotten off to a bad start, that he could straighten things out in no time. He hadn't expected the fifth grade to be so hard. It was really, really hard!

When he realized we were immune to his excuses, lame as they were, he said that what we were doing wasn't fair because we hadn't warned him.

"You know us, Eric," I said. "We don't warn. We *do*."

Four weeks later, we met with his teachers. They had almost forgotten our appointment. Eric had reminded them.

I began the conference by asking how Eric had fared over the past month. Unanimously, they told us that he'd been a completely changed child since the day after the last appointment. He had transformed himself into a model of responsibility and respect. There were no problems, nothing to discuss. Eric was a free man again.

□ □ □

One of the biggest problems in today's parenting culture is that parents are taking their marching orders from "experts" who would never recommend anything close to the approach Willie and I took to Eric's fifth-grade problems. Most of them, in fact, would be appalled at the thought. They would recommend some limp-wristed approach that would solve nothing. Then they would say that the limp wrist had solved nothing because the child in question had ADHD or some such drivel. I'm convinced, in fact, that many children end up with one diagnosis or another because so many of today's mental health professionals can't think outside the box of psychological correctness. What Willie and I did was most definitely not psychologically correct. It was along the lines of what our parents and parents of prior generations would have done under similar circumstances, 90 percent of which was not psychologically correct in the least, and 90 percent may be a conservative figure. In terms that were once part of America's parenting vernacular, after *giving him all the rope he needed to hang himself,* Willie and I lowered the boom on young Master Eric. Very old-fashioned stuff, that. Very "psychologically incorrect." Yet very effective. How often have you heard of ADHD being cured in thirty days?

To help Eric realize the wisdom of solving his classroom problem, Willie and I simply invoked the Agony Principle, which states:

The Agony Principle

Parents should not agonize over anything a child does or fails to do if the child is perfectly capable of agonizing over it himself.

We simply put the monkey of the problem on Eric's back. And it was a huge monkey. Like, King Kong.

Had Willie and I agreed to the teachers' well-intentioned recommendations—make sure he did his homework every night, check it, go over it with him—the monkey would have been clinging to *our* backs. The monkey is the embodiment of the Agony Principle. It motivates the person who's wearing it to solve the problem. So when parents wear the monkey, *they* are motivated to solve the problem. But Eric's behavior and school performance problems could only be solved by him. The same is true for most children's behavior problems. Parents and teachers can *support* a child's attempts to solve a problem, but they cannot solve it for the child. So if the problem, whatever it is, can only be solved by the child, and the wrong people are wearing the monkey, the problem is not going to get solved.

The fact that many of today's parents are wearing monkeys that belong on their kids' backs is perhaps the biggest reason that so many of today's kids get diagnosed with ADHD and other fictitious disorders.[6] These parents are always well-intentioned. Nonetheless, they are their own, and their children's, worst enemies.

Parents all over the USA ask me questions about problems they're having with their kids. The exchange often goes like this: Parents describe a behavior or school performance problem. I ask, "Who is upset because of this problem?" Parents reply, "Well, us, of course. *We're* upset." I reply, "In that case, the problem cannot be solved."

Having gotten their full attention, I proceed to tell them that the only person who can solve the problem—the only person who can decide to do his work and do his best in school, stop lying, stop teasing the family dog, be obedient, eat what's put on his plate, stop screaming at bedtime, stop smoking marijuana, whatever the problem—is the child in question. Then I explain the Agony Principle: the child will not solve the problem as long as the problem is upsetting other people and not himself. Assuming the parents see the wisdom of doing so, we then get down to crafting a Diabolical Plan guaranteed to cause the child great emotional distress.

Through this sort of counseling or coaching, I try to help people learn to be "stand-up" parents. Stand-up parenting is a rare thing these days, and if my ears are properly set to the ground, it's becoming rarer all the time. Parents stand up when they prove to their children they *mean* exactly what they say. In so doing, they become, in their children's eyes, "mean."

How to Become a Big Fat Meanie

A number of years ago, I had the opportunity to help a couple develop a stand-up parenting style while their first child was still a toddler. After the birth of their fourth child, they got back in touch to thank me for helping them have a happy parenthood. Then they related an incident that had taken place concerning their oldest, a boy. It's what stand-up parenting is all about.

Shortly after the school year began, their son's third-grade teacher told them he was talking excessively in class and not following her directions very well. My friends subsequently sat him down and told him that his participation in an upcoming field trip depended on his completely solving those problems. They made it perfectly clear that they were not willing to accept a partial solution.

Several days later, the teacher reported another incident. That evening, his parents told him he wasn't going on the field trip, which was still ten days away. As one might expect, he had a major meltdown, denying that his classroom behavior was a problem and threatening to become "really bad" if they didn't change their minds. They stood their ground.

"For the next ten days," wrote his mother, "we had the best-behaved son. The teacher even asked us to change our minds about the field trip, calling our attention to his greatly improved classroom behavior."

But these Big Fat Meanies didn't change their minds. They followed through as promised, telling me that if they hadn't, the whole exercise would have been a joke. Indeed, and a waste of everyone's time and energy. Since that watershed event, the boy's behavior has been sterling, both at home and at school.

His mother wrote, "The respect we saw after this one hard lesson was huge. He now knows that his dad and I are on the same page and that we don't say one thing and then do something else entirely."

I know there are folks out there who will think these parents went too far, that they should have reconsidered their ruling after the teacher's plea, and that in not doing so, they were being unreasonable—as in mean. I disagree, but then, I believe in being mean, as previously defined. Therefore, I completely support what these parents did. What they did is a perfect example of the Agony Principle in action.

The Agony Principle embodies the fact that children have to learn some lessons the hard way. For this little boy, this was one such lesson. Had his parents let him go on the field trip, he would have learned nothing of value. He would have learned, rather, that when he gets himself in trouble, he can get himself out of it by playing contrite. He would have learned, in short, to be manipulative, to play games. Instead, he learned that when his parents lay down the law, he needs to pay close attention. In fact, he learned that he needs to make sure things never get to the point where his parents feel the need to lay down the law, because once they do, they are going to follow through.

This little guy's parents are throwbacks, for sure, by which I mean that they would have felt more at home fifty-plus years ago, when stand-up parenting was the norm. For example, when my parents told me, in January 1960, that one more report of misbehavior from any of my teachers would result in me repeating the seventh grade, excellent grades notwithstanding,

I believed them. The next day, and for the rest of the year, I held my "ADHD with overtones of several other behavior disorders" in check. To this day, I absolutely know they would have held me back. Stories of that sort are not unusual in my generation. It's unfortunate that today's kids, by and large, are deprived of the same degree of certainty in their lives.

In that regard, it is a fact that today's kids are not as happy or as care-free as kids were in the 1950s. Childhood depression, once a relatively rare thing, verges on epidemic today. The irony is that the 1950s child was held to higher standards at home and at school, and the 1950s parent was almost universally a Big Fat Meanie.

I have to believe that there's a correlation between Big Fat Meanie parents and happy children. The research proves as much. It says that the happiest, most well-adjusted children are also the best-behaved children. That doesn't happen by accident.

How to Become a Big Fat Meanie, Part Two

Here are more real-life examples of the healing properties of the Agony Principle, complete with case examples and responses, also known as Diabolical Plans:

> **Case:** Just-turned-four-year-old girl refuses to use the toilet. Tells her parents she likes wearing diapers.
>
> **Diabolical Plan:** Said diaper-addict is confined to the bathroom for three days, sans diapers. She lives in the bathroom. She eats her meals in the bathroom. She has two dolls to play with in the bathroom. She is told that if she has an "on purpose" while in the bathroom, her three days will start over again.
>
> **Outcome:** Four-year-old girl is out of the bathroom in three days, and never fails to use the toilet properly again. Much to no one's surprise, she is a much happier child after her solitary confinement (during which time her life was still better than the lives of most of the world's children). Oppositional defiant disorder with toilet phobia cured in three days!

Case: Ten-year-old is a constant behavior problem in school. He disrupts the class, openly talks back to his teachers, and is a verbal bully on the playground.

Diabolical Plan: Budding sociopath comes home from school one day to discover that there is nothing in his room but a bed, chest of drawers, desk, lamp, and *essential* clothing, and the essential clothing in question is decidedly uncool. He is told that he must have no problems for a month, thirty days straight, after which time he will begin to get his stuff back, one thing at a time, beginning with the item he wants back the least and going up the line from there—one flawless day, one thing back. Any problem during the thirty days and the thirty days start over. Any problem after the thirty days, during his "parole," and all his stuff is taken away and the plan gets reset to square one.

Outcome: Child threatens to call child protection services. Parents hand him the phone, look up the number, and tell him to be their guest. He has second thoughts. He throws a full-blown bipolar tantrum, during which he kicks his bed apart. His parents remove the broken bed, put his mattress on the floor, and say nothing. For a week, nothing changes. Then, slowly, his behavior begins to improve. Six months later, after several resets, he has all his stuff back and is obviously a much happier child.[7]

Case: Sixteen-year-old boy gets arrested for shoplifting. He has no prior arrests, but he has been hanging with a bad bunch of boys and his behavior over the past year has been deteriorating, including treating his parents with great disrespect.

Diabolical Plan: He wakes up one Saturday morning to find that his car has disappeared. His parents tell him that when he rids himself of the demons he has allowed to possess him, and is completely demon-free for six months—new friends, respectful of others, responsible, and trustworthy—they will go get his car out of storage.

Outcome: Six months later, the parents get his car out of storage. A year later, he is still on the wagon, where he'll likely stay.

In each of these cases, parents responded to the problem by invoking the Agony Principle. Instead of getting upset, they acted such that the child became upset. Because the monkey was on the child's back, the child solved the problem.

The Godfather Was a Parenting Expert!

The Agony Principle is a concept that simply says that when a child does something bad, the *child* should feel bad about it. Because their consciences are not fully developed, children do not naturally feel bad about bad things they do. They need outside agents, therefore, to make them feel bad. That's where adults—parents and teachers—come in. Bringing the Agony Principle to bear on a child requires that the adults in the misbehaving child's life bring into play what I call the Godfather Principle (thanks due to Don Vito Corleone):

The Godfather Principle

To activate the Agony Principle, you simply make the misbehaving, irresponsible child *an offer he can't refuse.*

To illustrate what I'm talking about here, let's go back to the story of my son, Eric. Imagine that instead of confining Eric to his room for a month, Willie and I had only taken away his television privileges. At the end of that month, I guarantee his teachers would have reported minimal progress, if any at all, because taking away television alone would not have reflected the Godfather Principle: it would not have been an offer Eric could not refuse. It would have occasionally annoyed him that he couldn't watch a particular program, but he would have quickly adjusted to the inconvenience. It would have been the equivalent of your boss telling you that because you are late to work every day he is going to take away your morning coffee break or move your desk away from the window. Eric "woke up" because the wake-up call we gave him was *huge*. Being confined to his room and going to bed at seven o'clock for a month was no minor inconvenience. It amounted to the most terrible, horrible thing he could possibly have imagined. He never, ever wanted that to happen again.

That was proven two years later. In October of his seventh-grade year in school, his first year in junior high school, he and I were in the car and he told me he probably wasn't going to get a good grade in English.

"Why not?" I asked.

"Dad," he replied with great angst, "my teacher doesn't like me."

I pulled over in the first available parking area so that I could give this conversation my full attention.

"Explain that."

"Well, Dad, she just doesn't like me. She ridicules me when I answer a question in class; she marks all over my papers in red; she blames me for things I haven't done. She just doesn't like me at all, and Dad, I'm trying my best, I really am!"

"How many kids are there in this English class?" I asked, acting genuinely concerned, when in fact I had a good idea what the real story was.

"I don't know," he answered. "Maybe, um, thirty."

"So she doesn't like thirty kids?"

He looked at me with decidedly perplexed expression, then said, "No. She just doesn't like me and one other kid."

"Two out of thirty," I mused. "That means she likes twenty-eight of the kids in the class. That means that two kids in her class are making it difficult for her to do her job, and you're one of the two."

"No! Dad! I'm not making it difficult—"

I cut him off. "Eric, I've been there, done that. You can't pull this piece of wool over your daddy's eyes, so don't waste your breath. You and one other kid have decided to have a little fun with this teacher. That's unacceptable."

I paused for dramatic effect and then said, "Do you remember the fifth grade?"

His face exploded in shock. "The month in my room?! Dad! You can do that to a kid, but I'm not a kid anymore! I'm in the seventh grade! I'm nearly thirteen years old! You can't put a thirteen-year-old in his room for a month!"

After his outburst had run its course, I calmly said, "Right. In the fifth grade it was a month. That was two years ago. In the seventh grade, it's three months, or one whole grading period."

"Three months! Dad! You have to be kidding!"

"Do I look like I'm kidding?" I asked. "I think not. Eric, you had better make a B in English, and you had better not have a bad behavior report from your teacher, or you will be in your room for the entire next grading period. I'm simply not going to accept that you are making it difficult for a teacher to do her job."

It goes without saying that he began pleading and offering all manner of excuses, but I calmly pulled back on the road and continued to our intended destination.

Eric's report card came out just before Thanksgiving. He had made a B in English. In the comments section, the teacher had written "Eric's attitude and behavior made a remarkable turnaround midway through this grading period. I hope he keeps it up!"

The point of the story is that by confining Eric to his room for a month in the fifth grade, we not only helped him solve an immediate problem but also set a disciplinary precedent that helped him solve a problem two years later. Because of what Willie and I did when he was in the fifth grade, Eric absolutely knew that we would keep him in his room for three months in the seventh grade. What did he value more than anything else? What was the "currency" of his standard of living? One word: *freedom*. Therefore, the Godfather—in this case, me—simply made it clear that he was willing, once again, to severely curtail Eric's freedom.

One of the morals of all of these real-life stories, Eric's included, is that the only consequences worth delivering are *big* ones, ones that constitute a *huge* wake-up call, ones that instill *permanent* memories. Anything less is a waste of everyone's time. If you're having a problem with this sort of "put the hammer down" approach to discipline problems, just ask yourself, *Who is the primary beneficiary in each of the previous stories?* The answer, of course, is the child! Therefore, you should do whatever it takes to help your child solve his or her problems as quickly and as permanently as possible. You probably know some disobedient, disrespectful children. Do they seem like happy campers to you? No, they do not. They have dark clouds hanging around them. Do you know any obedient children who don't seem like happy campers? No, you don't. Obedience and happiness go hand in hand. No better source than the Bible tells us so:

> No discipline seems pleasant at the time, but painful. Later on, however, it produces a harvest of righteousness and peace for those who have been trained by it. (Hebrews 12:11)

The Godfather Cures a Child's Bedtime "Fears"

The parents of seven-year-old Philip sought my help with his bedtime fears. He insisted that one of his parents stay with him until he fell asleep. If they balked, he would cry and scream until they gave in. They tried reasoning with him, letting him "cry it out," bribes of various sorts, even the imaginative approach. They'd read an article that recommended giving fearful children water pistols filled with "monster repellent" (water spiked with cheap aftershave lotion) with which to defend themselves at night. But Philip wasn't a preschooler, and the imaginative approach flopped as well.

I suggested that Philip be given the "monkey" of the problem and, therefore, the opportunity to tame the monkey. If he wanted one of his parents to stay with him until he was asleep, a parent would stay with him. The next day, however, Philip paid the price by not being allowed to watch television or play his video games and going to bed one hour early. His parents left it completely up to him whether or not he wanted a companion at bedtime, but if he wanted to keep his privileges, he had to solve his problem. It was, after all, a problem only *Philip* could solve. Before this, Philip's parents wrestled with the monkey of his bedtime fears, and the more they wrestled with the monkey, the stronger and more persistent the monkey got.

For several weeks after his parents invoked the Agony and Godfather Principles, nothing changed. Philip continued to request that a parent lie down with him at bedtime. At first, he said he didn't care if he lost privileges the next day. By the second week, however, he was visibly upset at losing privileges and was tearfully begging his parents to lighten up. When they expressed concern, I pointed out that things usually got worse before getting better. Sure enough, three weeks into the program, Philip suddenly announced he didn't want any more company at bedtime.

"I'm mad at you," he told his parents, to which they said, "That's all right, Philip. If you're mad at us, and you don't want us to lie down with you at bedtime, we understand. Call us if you change your mind."

That night was the first night of Philip's new life, a life free of bedtime fears. At least, if he continued to have a few fears, he didn't tell anyone. He handled them himself, which is what growing up is all about.

The Godfather Cures a Pigsty

Twelve-year-old Samantha's parents were at wits' end. Sam's room was like Fibber McGee's closet. Her parents, though, called it a "pigsty." It was strewn with toys, dolls, clothes, shoes, schoolwork, books, CDs, and things that could not even be identified. Her parents had tried everything they could think of to get her to keep her room clean. She, however, pointed out to them that it was *her* room and she should be allowed to keep it in whatever state *she* chose. They were confused.

"Is she right?" they asked me.

"You have to be kidding," I said, and went on to point out that Sam's room was not *hers* to do with as she pleased. Allowing her that prerogative at age twelve would set a precedent that could very possibly come back to haunt them during her teen years.

"If it's her room," I asked, "then when she's sixteen and wants to have a naked romp in there with her boyfriend, are you going to allow it?"

"Of course not!" they replied.

"Right! Even though she has use of the room, *you* set the standards concerning how she can use it."

They looked at one another as if lightbulbs were coming on. "Right!" they chorused.

"Then she has to keep the room she uses neat and clean according to your standards."

I told them to tell Sam that until she paid the share of the mortgage and the utility bills represented by her room, the room she called "her" bedroom was theirs, not hers. They would, however, let Sam use it. And if she kept it neat and clean according to their standards, they would let her have a door on her room.

Mom and Dad went into Sam's room and cleaned it according to their standards. Then they pointed out to Sam the details of what they had done so there could be no misunderstanding. Then they simply told her, "When the appearance of your room falls below this standard, one or both of us will come into your room while you're away from the house and clean it so it meets the standard again. As we leave your room, we will take your door off its hinges and lock it in the storage shed. If you keep your room neat and clean according to our standards for a week, you'll get your door back. If you keep it neat and clean for five days and then it slips below the standard, the week will start over when you bring it up to standard again."

Sam didn't think her parents would follow through on their "threat." It took less than twenty-four hours for her room to be a pigsty again. The next day, while Sam was at school, her mother cleaned her room. When she was finished, she took Sam's door off the hinges and put it in the garden shed, under lock and key.

When Sam came home from school, she threw a hissy-fit and threatened to run away. Then she threatened to call the local child abuse authority. Her parents told her to do whatever she felt she had to do to express her disdain at this injustice. Sam stewed for two days. Then she cleaned her room and kept it neat and clean for a week. Sam got her door back. A couple of weeks went by, during which time Sam's parents noticed that she was slowly but surely falling off the wagon. Little things began to pile up and become big things. It was obvious to them that Sam was pushing the envelope, so to speak.

So while Sam was at school, her mother cleaned her room again, took her door off its hinges, and locked it in the garden shed. Sam came home and hit the ceiling. She began screaming that she had kept her room clean and her parents weren't fair and she was going to run away and join the circus and so on and so forth. Her parents simply said, "We hope you get your door back in a week, but that's not up to us; it's up to you."

When Sam was finished with ranting, she went to her room and hung a blanket over her doorframe. Her parents were somewhat amused at her creativity. Every so often, when Sam was not home, they would peek behind the curtain. A week later, Sam came home from school to a room that had a door. And that was the end of that.

THE REFEREE'S RULE

Imagine that you're at a college basketball game. A foul is committed and the lead referee says to the offending player, "Now, look, I've had to get on to you about this sort of stuff before. This is the last warning I'm going to give you. Next time, watch out! I'm serious!" And with that, play resumes.

Several minutes later, another player commits a foul, and the referee yells, "All right! I've had enough of that from you! You're just a troublemaker! If you don't apologize to the other team for your behavior, I'm going to give them two free throws." The player promptly apologizes and play resumes.

Not long after, a player bangs into an opponent as he's about to make an easy basket. The ball goes wide of the net. The referee gets red in the face and yells, "How many times do I have to tell you not to do that?! What's that? You're sorry and you promise not to do it again? Well . . . I don't know. Huh? You'll wash my car after the game? Well, all right, but let's just try to be more careful next time."

Here's a one-question, multiple-choice test: what is going to happen if the referee continues to manage the game in that fashion?

a. The players get the message and stop committing fouls.
b. Everyone has a wonderful time because the referee is so forgiving.
c. The referee and players "bond" during the game and have great mutual respect for one another.
d. The fans like this new way of playing basketball so much that "old" basketball is never played again.
e. Within less than ten minutes, the game deteriorates into complete chaos.

The correct answer, of course, is c. Just kidding; it's e. The relevance of this story to our discussion has to do with the fact that most parents deal with disciplinary situations much like our referee. Instead of simply and matter-of-factly calling fouls and assessing penalties, parents are prone to warn, threaten, give second chances, assess punishments but fail to follow through, and make deals. If you see yourself in that description, then you already know that violating the Referee's Rule with children, as with basketball players, brings on chaos. Up until now, however, you probably thought that the disciplinary chaos in your household was being caused by your kids. I hope you now realize that *you're* causing the chaos, not them. Only when you arrive at that understanding can you correct the problem, whatever it is.

The Referee's Rule

When a child misbehaves, parents should not threaten, warn, give second chances, or make deals. They should simply and dispassionately call the "foul" and assess the penalty (in accordance with the Agony and Godfather Principles).

When children don't know when or if the proverbial ax is ever going to fall, they constantly test authority. Adhering to the Referee's Rule in your discipline will bring needed certainty into your children's lives. When they know beyond a shadow of a doubt that Mom and Dad mean exactly what they say, whether it's "pick up your toys now" or "you can't go outside right now," they will begin testing less and less. That means less whining, complaining, belligerence, crying, tantrums, begging, arguing, and any other form their testing takes.

Once again, we've discovered that the disciplinary problems you are dealing with in your home can be easily changed! How? You're going to change the *only* person whose behavior you can change: *yours!*

It can't be said often enough: *you cannot change your child's behavior.* You can only bring about circumstances in your child's life that will cause him to reconsider his behavior and change it himself. Because it is an impossible task, the attempt to change someone else's behavior, whether child or adult, brings on stress, anger, resentment, guilt, and a slew of other negative feelings. If you often experience those feelings concerning your child, don't despair. Better days are just around the corner!

One more thing: you may have recognized that the Referee's Rule is an operational definition of consistency. Being consistent enables your child to stop testing your authority. Most people think being consistent means doing the same thing every time a child misbehaves in a certain way. That's one form of consistency. But you can enforce rules consistently without doing the same thing every time a misbehavior occurs. Basketball referees have very few options when it comes to enforcing rules, but parents have lots of options. Parents, therefore, can be creatively "inconsistent" when it comes to consequences. In response to the same misbehavior from a child, parents can do five different things. What's important is that each of the five things embodies the Agony and Godfather Principles.

For example, I sometimes recommend that parents operate a "Consequence Lottery." Five to ten consequences are written on an equal number of slips of paper. The slips are then folded and put into a large jar or small goldfish bowl. For example:

- You must weed and pick up the yard until we approve of the job.
- You are confined to your room for the rest of the day.
- Your bedtime for the next three nights is at six thirty, lights out.
- You lose television and all other electronics for a week.
- Your friends cannot come over for two days, during which time you can't go to their houses either.
- You must clean all the bathrooms in the house—wash floors, scrub toilets, clean tubs and showers, and so on.
- Your bicycle is parked for the rest of the week.
- Other than school and worship services, you are confined to the house for three days.
- You cannot participate in any after-school activities for a week.
- Your cell phone is ours for a week.

When the child misbehaves, he must go to the jar or fish bowl, close his eyes, and draw a consequence. This method is recommended for kids who misbehave only occasionally. I call 'em "Low Misbehavers" or simply "LMs." They don't need to be on one of the structured discipline programs described in the next section—those are for children who frequently and flagrantly disobey. Nonetheless, when LMs misbehave, they should experience consequences just like everyone else. The point is, you can be consistent and authoritative without doing the same thing every time your child misbehaves. But the previous statement applies to LMs only. If your child is a High Misbehaver (HM), then before you can go to something like the "Consequence Lottery," you need to use one of the plans described in chapter 3 to transform your little HM into an LM.

THE PENICILLIN PRINCIPLE

The Penicillin Principle means pretty much the same thing as "Don't count your chickens before they hatch."

Let's say you come down with a bad case of strep throat. Your physician prescribes a ten-day regimen of an antibiotic, three pills a day. He stresses that you need to take the drug for the full ten days, whether you have symptoms or not.

A few days later, you are symptom free. Although you remember your physician's instructions, you begin slacking off. On the fourth day, you take two pills. On the fifth day, you take only one. Then you stop altogether. Two days later, you develop an even worse case of strep throat than you had before. When you call your physician, he tells you he's going to have to up the dose of antibiotic because a relapse is always a bigger challenge to treat. He also tells you that if you don't take the new dose for ten days, and you have another relapse, he's probably going to have to put you in the hospital.

The same principle applies to childhood behavior problems. Relapses are always more difficult to deal with than the original offense. And whether one is talking about a physical illness or a behavior problem, symptom relief always precedes the cure. They are not one and the same.

The Penicillin Principle

Don't confuse symptom relief with cure. If you abandon a successful discipline treatment at the point of symptom relief, the possibility of relapse is greatly increased. And a relapse is always more difficult to treat than the original condition.

When parents tell me that a particular discipline strategy worked for several weeks and then stopped working, I immediately suspect that the truth is as follows: "We worked at the strategy for several weeks and then, thinking we'd solved the problem, we stopped working at it." In other words, they confused symptom relief with cure.

But let's further extend the pharmaceutical analogy: When a person begins taking an antibiotic for any infection, the weaker germs are killed off first. The strongest ones are always the last ones to go. If the patient stops treatment before finishing the full course of the antibiotic, the strongest germs remain. In addition, the illness has left the patient temporarily weakened. The combination of strong germs and a weak patient is a prime environment for a relapse that is far more intense and, therefore, more resistant.

Likewise, when parents abandon a successful discipline strategy at the point of symptom relief, they maximize the possibility of a relapse. (Come to think of it, that's wrong. Under those circumstances, a relapse is inevitable!) And because the child now has reason to believe that his parents are not going to follow through completely, he's going to put up more of a fight this time around. In effect, their lack of commitment has strengthened him.

The usual course of a behavior problem, once an effective treatment plan has started, looks like this:

Week	Problem Status
1 Things get worse before they get better	Your child has received news of her punishment. Her ability to remain at the center of attention in (therefore, in control of) your family is now threatened. This provokes an increase in the strength of her behavior problem(s) as she struggles to keep things the way they have been.
2 The "honeymoon" phase	Your child begins to outwardly cooperate with the new program in the expectation that if she shows improvement, your enforcement will slack off. Your child most likely comes by this expectation honestly.
3 A second testing phase	The behavior problem escalates dramatically as your child does everything in her power to get you to abandon the plan.
4–11 Symptom relief	This is the beginning of lasting behavior change—if you stick with the program. Your child begins to realize that you mean business and are in this for the long haul. She begins to cooperate with the new plan, and her behavior problem slowly but surely begins to diminish and be replaced by prosocial behaviors.
12 Cure!	The behavior problem has been all but eradicated and replaced with, not just more functional behavior, but a visibly better attitude and self-concept as well. The family is effectively "out of the woods."

Note in the previous table that it generally takes three to four weeks of steady resolve and consistency before lasting, positive behavior change begins to take place. But that marks symptom relief only! Week 3 or 4 is the equivalent of the third or fourth day of a ten-day antibiotic prescription. It's the point at which relapse becomes most likely and can only be prevented if parents continue to enforce the new plan with a calm sense of purpose.

I am reminded of a family I worked with a number of years ago. The HM in this case was an eleven-year-old I'll call Eddie, because that was his real name. Eddie's parents told me he was their "curse." The Curse That Was Eddie began his reign of terror before he turned two. At eleven, he still acted like a toddler in most respects—at home, that is. At school, Eddie was a model student, which is why his teachers were amazed when Eddie's parents described the misbehavior they were dealing with: defiance, relentless picking on his much-younger siblings, and full-blown tantrums when he didn't get his way.

I recommended to Eddie's parents that they begin the Curse's rehabilitation by first stripping his room down to a bed, chest of drawers, desk, lamp, and essential clothing. I call that being "Kicked Out of the Garden of Eden" (see full description in chapter 3). Once they'd reduced Eddie's standard of living to essentials only, I had them implement a process I call "Strikes" (also described in chapter 3). Any act of defiance (including ignoring them when they spoke to him), verbal aggression toward his siblings, or even the slightest of tantrums resulted in the parent on the scene of the crime calling a "strike." Nothing else happened. After calling the strike, the parent simply walked away. (Note: They did not press the issue, which probably would have resulted in another strike, and then another. That would have done nothing but infuriate Eddie and convince him there was no way he could "beat the system," in which case the system would have created an even bigger problem.) When Eddie incurred his third strike on any given day, he was sent to his room for the rest of the day, a room which had previously been a paradise of toys and electronics but was now about as Spartan as a military barracks. On the refrigerator, his parents posted a thirty-block grid. Every day that Eddie incurred only one or two strikes, his parents filled in one of the blocks on the grid with a smiley face. When he had earned smiley faces for thirty straight days, his room would be restored to its previous glory. If Eddie earned smiley faces for, let's say, fifteen straight days and on day sixteen incurred a third strike, his parents took down the existing thirty-block grid, threw it away, and put up a new one.

At first, Eddie rebelled. His behavior worsened considerably, proving the adage that things get worse before they get better. His parents hung in there, helped along by frequent phone conversations with me.

For the first several weeks, Eddie tested the system, then honeymooned with it, then tested it again. Then he began to settle down, and it was obvious that he was trying to reform himself. After numerous failures over four weeks' time, Eddie finally managed to get to day five of a thirty-day chart. He got to day fifteen on the next one. He got to day seventeen on the next one. Then, success! Thirty blocks, thirty smiley faces! If you do the math, you find that it took Eddie four weeks to get to the point where he was no longer actively testing his parents' resolve. That's symptom relief, effectively. It took him nearly ten more weeks (sixty-seven days) before he was fully cured.

When it was all over and I talked to Eddie about what he'd been through, he told me, "I don't ever want that to happen again. At first, I didn't think it was fair. I hated you, and I hated my parents. But I know it was good for me. I'm a better person. It's like I had some infection or something and I don't have it anymore."

That's pretty impressive stuff coming from the mouth of an eleven-year-old.

Generally speaking, it takes about twice as long to get the cure as it takes to get to symptom relief (when the misbehavior pretty much disappears). In Eddie's case, symptom relief took four weeks, which is typical. His cure came an additional eight weeks later. But one could legitimately say that Eddie was really cured by the second week of his last thirty-day chart. The last two weeks were icing on the cake.

In some cases, however, complete symptom relief may take only a couple of weeks, in which case cure should be achieved by week six (another four weeks). Even if symptom relief takes place in just one week, which sometimes happens, I usually recommend no less than a six-week length of treatment. Relapses after the point of cure are unusual, but they do take place. In most cases, they are not "full-blown" and can be successfully handled by putting the child back on the plan for a week or two.

A mom writes: "Obviously, this isn't easy. It's going to be annoying and frustrating at times to stay on top of discipline after a day of changing diapers, cooking meals, cleaning house, going on play dates or errands, etc. It's easier to just say, 'Fine! Go watch television.' Discipline is not easy, but that's the point. Parents taking the easy way out is causing so many problems in our culture. If you do this early enough and consistently enough, you'll have obedient children and parenting will be much easier down the road." Well said!

BITE OFF ONLY WHAT YOU CAN CHEW

A parent e-mailed me this question: "My four-year-old ignores me, defies me, talks back, throws tantrums, lies, steals things from us and his grandparents, is disruptive in restaurants and other public places, leaves his possessions strewn all over the house, starts fights with his older siblings, and teases the family dog relentlessly. What should I do?"

My answer: "Take a deep breath, relax, and instead of trying to take ten steps (the ten behavior problems identified) in one reckless bound, take those ten steps one step at a time." I went on to suggest that since it was probably the easiest problem to deal with, she should begin her son's rehabilitation by working to eliminate disruptions in public places, and then told her how to accomplish that (see pages 33–37). She wrote me a few weeks later saying, "I did what you said and his problems in public disappeared in a week. The amazing thing, however, is that several other problems have also disappeared, including teasing the dog, and I did nothing about them!"

Generally speaking, the more intense your child's behavior problems, the more frustrated you are; and a frustrated parent is likely to try to bite off much, much more than he can possibly chew, thus dooming any discipline plan to failure before it even starts.

If your child's behavior problems are legion, you would do well to not try to deal with more than two or three distinct problems at any one time, five at the most if your child is elementary-school age. In some cases, and especially with preschool children, one problem may be enough to fill your plate. Start with the behavior issue that you feel will be easiest to fix and work from there, tackling a new misbehavior after the previous one has been cured. By starting with the easiest problem, you increase the likelihood of early success. A positive outcome will translate to a positive attitude, and leadership—the primary theme of this chapter—is all about a positive attitude.

As testified to by the mom in the previous vignette, early disciplinary success also has a positive effect on the child. Notice that when Mom focused on and solved the issue of her son's misbehavior in restaurants and other public places, his behavior in other settings began to improve. She did nothing about his relentless teasing of the family dog, for example, but the teasing stopped along with the public disruptions. If, on the other hand, she had tried to deal with every one of his misbehaviors at once, she would have bitten off more than she could have chewed. She would have further frustrated herself, experienced further failure, and her son's behavior might well have worsened.

There are, however, ways of dealing with a host of problems all at once. One such approach, "Kicking Out of the Garden of Eden," was integral to Eddie's rehabilitation (see pages 58–59), and is described in detail in chapter 3. Keep in mind, however, that no matter the strategy, a calmly authoritative parental attitude is required. Highly frustrated parents who are at the end of their emotional ropes are not likely to get any discipline strategy to work.

THE JEREMIAH PRINCIPLE

Twice in the biblical book of Jeremiah, God laments through His prophet that nothing He has done has succeeded at causing the Israelites, His chosen people (one might substitute His most cherished children), to listen to and obey Him.

> Yet they did not listen or pay attention; they were stiff-necked and would not listen or respond to discipline. (17:23)

> They turned their backs to me and not their faces; though I taught them again and again, they would not listen or respond to discipline. (32:33)

Sounds like the early Israelites suffered collectively from attention-deficit hyperactivity disorder and oppositional defiant disorder—or, ADHD and ODD. Perhaps God should have given them daily doses of some psychiatric drug—laced their water supply with it, for instance. Instead of manna, medication from heaven. What a concept!

But seriously, when God created us, He gifted us with free will, the ability to make autonomous decisions. Interestingly enough, God has set things up such that He can influence us, but He cannot control us (it's probably more accurate to say that He *can* control us but has chosen not to). Likewise, you can influence your children, but you cannot control them. Fifty-plus years ago, when people saw children through the clarifying lens of common sense, parents knew that every child has a mind of his own. They knew, in other words, that their best efforts to discipline their children might fail.

Your Child Is the Decider

Today's parents believe in psychology, the worldview of which embraces a cause-and-effect determinism. Psychology proposes that parenting determines how a child behaves and ultimately turns out—in other words, that parenting *produces* the child. That's why, if you go see a psychologist about a problem you're having in your life, the likelihood is that the good doctor will help you explore your childhood memories. Thus seeking a cause for your present psychic discomfiture, he will find one. He will, in a great "Aha!" moment, connect some "trauma" or unresolved issue in your childhood with your present problem.

According to psychology, bad parenting produces or leads to bad or dysfunctional adult behavior, and good parenting produces good or functional adult behavior. But common sense says that's just not so. Some kids raised in good families do really, really bad or just downright stupid things (and don't seem to learn from their mistakes), and some kids raised in really bad families turn out well. Contrary to the psychological myth, parenting does not produce the child. That is extremely important for today's parents to understand and accept, so I'll say it again, with special emphasis: *parenting does not produce the child*! Parenting is an influence, and your job is to maximize the positive aspects of your influence. But in the final analysis, your child takes your influence and—read this carefully—*he decides what he's going to do with it*. It's all about free will, the ability to choose what the serpent tells us to do over what God tells us to do.

The Child Produces Himself, Exhibit A

In 1995, Timothy McVeigh blew up a federal building in Oklahoma City, killing 168 people. He was unrepentant until the end. His parents divorced when he was ten, but that doesn't explain premeditated mass murder, including numerous preschool children. After all, my parents divorced when I was three. It would be impossible to draw a straight line from any feature of McVeigh's childhood to his actions leading up to and on April 19, 1995. McVeigh, not his parents or the kids he claimed bullied him as a child (I was bullied too—relentlessly, in fact—and I have no "unresolved anger issues" that I need to vent by doing harm to people or their possessions), blew up that building and killed those people. Nothing about his childhood made his actions inevitable. He is completely, 100 percent responsible for his crime.

When I am speaking on this topic, I remind my audience of the story contained in the third chapter of the book of Genesis. In summary, the Only Perfect Parent There Is or Ever Will Be creates two children who disobey His first instruction. In so doing, they commit the most heinous offense they could possibly have committed. If parenting produces the child, then what, pray tell, did God do to cause His first children to rebel against Him so blatantly? The answer, obviously, is God did nothing to cause the Fall. He gave His children every opportunity, every benefit, every right and proper thing, and they still managed to do the wrong thing.

In the end, *the child produces himself*. A child raised by parents who are good moral examples and provide good discipline may decide that he's going to use the good lessons he's learned to deceive and take financial advantage of people. That's why I often tell parents that they should never say, "My child would never [fill in the blank with some heinous behavior]." That's self-delusion. No matter how fine your parenting, your child is capable of doing bad stuff. If you accept that, then if and when bad stuff occurs, it won't throw you for a loop. You'll be able to deal with it from a state of balance. Likewise, a child raised in an abusive home by alcoholic parents may decide when he grows up that he's going to create an outreach ministry to families of that sort.

Proper discipline may cause a child to make better decisions. On the other hand, proper discipline of the sort described in this book may make a child that much more determined to get his own way. The frustrating thing is that it's impossible to determine, in advance, which child is going to react in which way. One thing is certain: if God's discipline has been rejected by His children, then your discipline may be rejected by your children as well.

The Jeremiah Principle

Proper discipline does not guarantee proper behavior.

"So John," a worried parent asks, "if I discipline properly, according to your old-fashioned ideas and principles, and my child keeps on misbehaving, what should I do then?"

You should keep right on doing the right thing. I've known of children who were stripped of all privileges and their most coveted possessions, and they still kept right on doing their bad things. That's just another form of rebellion. It's the child's defiant way of saying, "I don't care what you do to me! I'm king of my own life! No one has the power to tell the Almighty Me what to do! There is no authority in my life that supersedes my own!"

Most of these kids, thankfully, eventually come around. But not all of them do, and that is just the way it is when you're dealing with human beings instead of animals.

So the question becomes, what should parents do if a child refuses, no matter what, to come around?

My answer is they should love the child as much as they can, pray as hard as they can, do as little for the child as the law allows, and emancipate the child as soon as possible (perhaps into the military).

I am reminded of Jesus' parable of the prodigal son (Luke 15:11–32). The younger of a man's two sons takes his inheritance and goes off to a distant country where he wastes everything he has with "wild living." Eventually, he has to take work as a swineherd (given that pigs are unclean animals in Judaism, this is clear indication he's sunk to the bottom of the barrel). He finally comes to his senses, returns home, and throws himself on his father's mercy. Instead of giving him a stern lecture, his father greets him with open arms and throws a party. The older brother, who has always been good and faithful, complains to his father that he deserves the rewards, not his brother. The father replies that the older son's faithfulness is noted and will someday be rewarded, but the party will go on because "this brother of yours was dead and is alive again; he was lost and is found" (v. 32).

Like the father in Jesus' well-known parable, you may be called upon to let go of a rebellious child. If so, be assured that God will not give up on your child. Neither should you.

CHAPTER THREE

Seven Essential Tools

This is the chapter you've probably been waiting for with baited breath, the chapter in which I describe various structured approaches to corrective discipline. If you're like most parents, you think this chapter is the entrée, but it's not. The main course in this six-course meal is chapter 2, which you just read (and if you didn't, then I invoke the power vested in me as author to insist that you go back and read it right now!). Furthermore, the main feature on the plate of chapter 2 is Alpha Speech—the means by which parent authority is effectively conveyed. Take the present chapter out of context and you will bring down upon yourself the Ancient Curse of the Man Who Tried to Pull the Horse with the Cart, and an awful curse it is. Think of these techniques as vehicles for your authority. A technique is simply the form your authority takes. Also, the seven tools set forth herein are only examples of structured discipline plans. You are free to take them and be as creative with them as you like. It might even occur to you to invent a strategy no one's ever thought of before. Be my guest. Think outside the box!

A COMES BEFORE B

In March 2009, before I spoke to a large audience in Reno, Nevada, a woman came up to me in the lobby and told me she'd heard me talk three years prior. "I went home from that talk," she said, "and began using Alpha Speech. It was amazing! Within a month, my kids had gone from being brats to being well behaved again!"

Like that mother, parents who master Alpha Speech consistently report a 50 to 80 percent reduction in problem behaviors within two to four weeks. In this chapter, I describe structured approaches that parents can use with misbehaviors that remain—the most stubborn of the bunch. These tools will help parents organize their disciplinary behavior. Unorganized discipline is misdiscipline; it's incorrect and accomplishes nothing. Misbehavior on the part of children and misdiscipline on the part of parents almost always go hand in hand. Together, they create a vicious cycle of errors, one error feeding off the next, which feeds off the next, and so on.

Not all misbehavior, however, warrants a structured approach like "Tickets" or "Strikes." When a child's misbehavior isn't persistent, when it's occasional, using one of the structured interventions described in this chapter may wind up making a mountain out of a molehill. Overreaction to misbehavior causes its own set of problems.

High misbehavior of the sort that requires a punitive, consequence-based response generally falls into one or more D-word categories: disrespect, defiance (including passive forms of defiance, like ignoring), disruptiveness, destructiveness (including damage to property and aggression toward others), and deceit (lying and stealing). This is not to say that behavior that falls into one of those categories necessarily *requires* an organized plan of the sort I will lay out in this chapter. A shift of parenting style, characterized primarily by the use of Alpha Speech, has cured many a disrespectful, defiant, disruptive, destructive, and/or deceitful child. But no matter how effectively they project their leadership, parents will sometimes need to fall back to "Plan B": consequences. When consequences are called for, an organized approach of the sort described in this chapter will help you stay on track and telegraph your commitment to your child.

This chapter presents a number of successful disciplinary interventions—consequence delivery systems, if you will—along with real-life examples of how parents have used them to solve persistent and sometimes *big* behavior problems.

TICKETS

I developed "Tickets" in response to the observation that time-out only works with children who are already fairly well behaved. (Then again, just about any demonstration of parental disapproval will work with children who generally walk the straight and narrow.) When it comes to children who misbehave fairly frequently—a good number of whom will not cooperate with the instruction to sit still in a chair for five minutes— you'll find that time-out only works temporarily, if at all. Time-out is simply not a powerful behavioral deterrent, and only powerful messages get through to High Misbehavers.

Tickets sends a much more powerful message than time-out and is generally a good place to start a three- to thirteen-year-old child's rehabilitation process (as well as your own). I don't recommend Tickets (or any of the other strategies in this chapter, for that matter) with children who are younger than three or older than twelve. Two-year-olds don't think ahead. Consequently, they are too impulsive to predict consequences, which the success of a method like Tickets requires. With teens, a structured approach of this sort may provoke an upsurge in misbehavior, especially defiance. Tickets has brought about positive outcomes with a very select number of thirteen- and fourteen-year-olds, but the decision to use it with that age child needs to be made prudently.

To begin using Tickets, you'll need: a refrigerator magnet, a magnetic clip, three to five "tickets" (two-by-five-inch rectangles cut from colored construction paper[1]), and a list of target misbehaviors—misbehaviors that you are "targeting" for elimination.

It's very important that you specify your child's target misbehaviors in terms that are concrete rather than abstract. "Being disrespectful to

Sample Target Misbehaviors List

1. Refusing to do what we tell you to do.
2. Yelling at us when we tell you no.
3. Teasing the dog.
4. Jumping on furniture.
5. Sneaking food into your room.

us" is an example of the latter and will only cause a child to have to engage in a longer period of testing in order to find out what "being disrespectful" actually means. In this case, it will be helpful to all concerned if the target is "Calling us names, like 'stupid' or 'dumb.'" For children who are not yet able to read, simple drawings such as the ones shown below (don't be concerned about artistic quality—stick figures will do) can substitute for word descriptions. However, if parents are consistent with enforcement, this level of concreteness won't be necessary. With repetition, even a young three-year-old will quickly figure out what his or her target misbehaviors are.

Jumping on Furniture

Refusing to Obey

In most cases, and especially with three-, four-, and five-year-olds, I recommend starting with one target behavior (in picture form or in bold print on an index card) and five tickets. When the initial misbehavior is pretty well under control and has been for at least a week, a second target can be added to the list. When that's under control, you can add a third, and so on. Even with an older child who is High Misbehaver, I strongly encourage you to resist the temptation to try to eliminate every misbehavior at once. If you let your frustration and impatience get the better of you, you are likely to make matters worse instead of better. With a child older than five, start with no more than three misbehaviors that can be clearly identified.

A mother recently asked if she could put "general disrespect" on the target list. When I asked her to be more specific, she said when she reprimanded her eleven-year-old daughter, the child often grinned and/or rolled her eyes.

I said, "Your daughter is trying to tell you that you're using too many words. You're talking too much, going needlessly on and on and on with a lot of yada-yada."

The mother looked at me for several seconds and said, "You're absolutely right."

I said, "Been there, done that."

"So," she said, "you're saying that particular misbehavior is my fault."

"Right, but I'd say it's your 'doing' as opposed to your 'fault.' Therefore, it should not be on the list." I further suggested to her that she make a Target Misbehavior List for herself and put "Yada-yada" at the top.

Things like eye-rolling and grinning are static, white noise. They are not the real problem. Furthermore, they are often (more often than not, in fact) understandable reactions to parents who get bad cases of "motormouth" when their kids misbehave. Ignore them and they generally go away.

At this point I need to say something *VERY IMPORTANT*: Just as you can micromanage a child's homework or social life or after-school time, you can micromanage a child's discipline. In whatever context, micro-management creates problems. Sometimes, as is the case when parents micromanage homework, the problem doesn't show up until later (in the form of a dependent child who does not think he or she is capable of solving problems without other people's help). When parents micromanage discipline by picking and harping on static like eye-rolling, they provoke even more insolence and defiance. So ignore this stuff (stop saying this stuff!):

- eye-rolling ("Don't you dare get that look on your face!")
- slumped body posture ("Stand up straight when I talk to you!")
- lack of eye contact ("Look at me when I talk to you!")
- grinning ("Wipe that grin off your face, young lady!")
- incredulous facial expression ("Don't act like you don't know what I'm talking about!")

Affix your Target Misbehavior List to the refrigerator with a magnet.[2] The tickets are put in the magnetic clip, then stuck on the refrigerator, right above or alongside the Target Misbehavior List.

Hold on; I see I have a question.

Q: How many tickets should I start with, John?

A: I generally recommend starting with no more than three clearly defined target behaviors and five tickets per day. With three-year-olds, however, start with one target behavior and five tickets. Having too many targets is overwhelming; too many tickets and the program becomes meaningless.

The Procedure: Every time the child exhibits one of his target misbehaviors . . .

1. The parent closest to the scene takes the child to the refrigerator, points to the appropriate item on the list, and says (for example), "Teasing the dog is on your list, which means I'm taking [or you're losing] a ticket."
2. The parent takes a ticket out of the clip and places it on top of the refrigerator.
3. (Optional) A time-out of five to fifteen minutes can also be enforced. If time-out is used, the location should be relatively isolated and the period should be defined by a timer as opposed to the parent saying, "You can get up now." If your child won't cooperate in time-out or has great difficulty sitting still for any period of time, either dispense

with it or simply tell him that he can trade his time-out for another ticket. ("If you'd rather not go to the time-out seat for ten minutes, that's fine. Just let me know and I'll take another ticket instead.") By the way, I know it seems like I'm contradicting myself here. I *did* say that time-out doesn't work. That's true, but let me be more specific: time-out doesn't work *by itself*. However, when it's used as a supplement to a program like Tickets, it can be very helpful, if only to give parent and child a "cooling off" period.

When the last ticket is taken, the child incurs a consequence or consequences. Not something small, mind you, like taking away his favorite toy or one privilege for the rest of the day. The consequence has to reflect the Agony and Godfather Principles. I usually recommend confining the child to his or her room for the remainder of the day (he can come out to use the bathroom, eat meals with the family, do chores, and leave the house with the family if there's no option) and putting him to bed at least one hour earlier than usual. For obvious reasons, I recommend that the "play value" of the child's room be significantly reduced during his rehabilitation. The next day, all of the child's tickets are restored—the proverbial slate is wiped clean. *Do not carry unused tickets over to the following day*. For example, if your child's daily complement of tickets is five, and he loses only three one day, he still begins the next day with five tickets.

Obviously, all misbehaviors are not equal. Hitting you is certainly more egregious than yelling, "You're a dummy!" Outrageous, highly antisocial behaviors—generally, those that are aggressive, hurtful, or destructive— should result in the loss of more than one ticket at a time. In fact, I recommend that any act of physical aggression—hitting, kicking, spitting— toward a parent, sibling, or pet results in the loss of all remaining tickets, regardless of whether the aggression hit the mark or not.

You can also "override" the program at your discretion. Say your child is working on three target misbehaviors and has five tickets per day. You receive a call from his fifth-grade teacher, who reports that he called her "stupid" in front of the class. The Tickets system could not possibly have anticipated this. You could take away all of your child's tickets for that day, but spending the rest of the after-school day in his room is not going to be an adequate response to an offense of that nature. So you override the program. In addition to making him write his teacher a letter of apology and read it in front of the class, you take away all of your child's privileges and confine him to his room (which you have stripped of "play value") for a week.

Parents Say It Works!

"I just want to say thanks for the idea of the Tickets System and encourage others to use it to eliminate unwanted behaviors. It's been a success with our three-year-old, stopping whining, tantrums, talking back, and saying no to us. He looks forward to getting his tickets every morning and playing the Ticket Game (which he always wins now!). He started being aggressive toward other kids at preschool. As you suggested, the school called me, I picked him up, and he stayed in his room the rest of the day and went to bed right after supper. He said, 'Mommy, that was not fun. I never want to do that again!' Since implementing your tactics, our son is so much happier, and so are we. Even his teachers have noticed and have commended us. Thanks so much."

The success of the program depends on you. In that regard, you absolutely must observe the Referee's Rule: no threats, warnings, or second chances (see pages 52–55). When your child misbehaves, it is essential that you not say things like, "Do you want to lose a ticket?" or, "If you don't do what I just told you to do, I'm going to take a ticket." Also, do not allow a child to earn back tickets with good behavior or acts of service. Lost is lost. If your child tries to bargain with you over lost tickets, saying, "If I'm good, will you give me a ticket back?" simply say, "No, because I expect you to be good."

As your child's behavior improves, the number of daily tickets can be gradually reduced so as to keep pressure on him or her to continue making progress. Or you can add misbehaviors, one at a time, to the target list. Do not, however, add targets and reduce tickets at the same time. Do one or the other. When your child has managed to keep his misbehaviors under control for three to four weeks, it's time to see how he will do off the program. Generally speaking, full rehab, from start to finish, takes six to twelve weeks, after which your child will be perfectly behaved, forever. (My editor has compelled me to admit that those last nine words constitute a gross exaggeration. She also took one of my tickets. I'll do better, I promise.)

Parents Say It Works!

"I have a normally very obedient three-year-old daughter, but lately I've had several problems with disrespect and disobedience. After one extremely stressful day with her, I remembered the Tickets System, which I had done with her about a year ago. The next day I posted three target misbehaviors. She lost all her tickets by that afternoon and went to her room. By the next day her behavior had drastically improved and has been much better since. I discontinued it after a week. I know that the Tickets System usually takes longer and was probably started for more long-term problems, but I just wanted to share how it can also be used for issues that are more temporary. It's just a good way to be more matter-of-fact and less emotional about misbehavior. Thanks so much!"

Q & A

Q: Can I use Tickets to deal with misbehavior that occurs away from home?

A: Absolutely. One of the advantages of Tickets is it's portable. Say, for example, that your four-year-old misbehaves in the car or a store. You can simply say, "Refusing to do what I tell you to do is on your list. When we get home, you will lose a ticket and sit for fifteen minutes in time-out."

You can also use Tickets to deal with nothing but

misbehavior that occurs in public places. Before going into a public situation with your child—a store, for example—stop and say something along this line: "The rules in stores are very simple. First, you stay with me unless I have given you permission to leave my side for some reason. Second, you don't touch anything without my permission. Third, do not interrupt me when I'm talking with someone else."

At that point, you hand over three to five tickets (the actual number is a judgment call based on the child's age, the length of time you'll be in the store, and the history of the problem) and say, "These tickets are going to help you remember the rules. Every time you break one of the rules, I'm going to take a ticket away from you. When we get home, you must have at least one ticket left in order to enjoy your privileges for the rest of the day. If you lose all of your tickets in the store, then you will not be allowed to go outside, watch television, or play video games for the rest of the day, and I will put you to bed right after supper."

Having a discipline plan enables you to keep your balance, your cool, when a problem occurs. In the past, when your child darted away from you in a store or put his fingers on an expensive breakable item, you became instantly flustered. Now, however, you simply remind him of the rule and take a ticket.

The punitive consequence can be anything your child is looking forward to doing later in the day, but again, it should be a privilege. Do not offer him a reward for behaving properly in public (this applies to proper behavior in any context). Contrary to what most people think, and as I've said in chapter 1, rewards are not effective motivators. The best way to use rewards is to surprise, rather than bribe. For example, if your child behaves exceptionally well in a store and keeps all, or most of, his tickets, you can (but are not obligated to) honor the achievement with a surprise ice-cream cone. But beware!

Don't do this so often that he comes to expect a reward, or you just might undo what Tickets has helped you accomplish.

STRIKES

"Strikes" is a variation on Tickets for children six and older. You still need a short list of target misbehaviors, posted on the refrigerator or bulletin board, but instead of taking a ticket when a target misbehavior occurs, you simply call a *strike*, as in "You're ignoring me. That's strike one." The first misbehavior of the day is strike one, and so on. At the outset of the program, you give your child a daily allowance of three to five strikes. Again, the actual number is a judgment call. Once again, you can elect to have your child sit in time-out each time he incurs a strike.

Obviously, and as is also the case with Tickets, you're going to give your child a margin of error where misbehavior is concerned. For example, if you give your child five strikes a day, then the first four constitute his margin of error—he can misbehave four times a day without penalty (other than time-out, if you've elected to use it). We're not going to expect perfection here. Nobody's perfect, or even comes close.

When your child uses his last strike of the day, he's "out," meaning he experiences some meaningful consequence like being confined to his room for the remainder of the day without electronic diversions and going to bed at least one hour early. As is the case with Tickets, I generally recommend that the "play value" of the room be considerably reduced by removing favorite playthings.

Obviously, Strikes is a bit easier to administer than Tickets, but that same quality also lends itself to sloppiness or immoderation where enforcement is concerned. Sloppiness occurs when you forget to call strikes when misbehaviors occur, and you fall slowly back into old bad habits. Immoderation is at the opposite extreme; it occurs when you begin calling strikes over minutiae, such as the expression on your child's face. If you decide to use Strikes, simply be aware of those pitfalls.

As your child's behavior improves, you can "up the ante" by either reducing your child's daily allotment of strikes or adding specific misbehaviors to the Target Misbehavior List. Don't do both! Do one or the other. If you begin with three target misbehaviors and five strikes (a four-strike margin of error), and within three weeks your child has that misbehavior pretty much under control, then you can either reduce his strikes to four per day (a three-strike margin of error) or add a new target. Don't ever reduce a child's daily allotment of either tickets or strikes to less than three.

It's definitely not a good idea to use Strikes with a child who averages numerous misbehaviors each day—an HM. The child's going to be in his room before nine o'clock in the morning! Several days of that is going to be demoralizing, and he is not going to see any point in trying to master the program. He's going to give up, in which case a very counterproductive precedent has been set. If you're struggling with an HM, keep reading—the next section has some helpful strategies for you!

CHARTS

Charts provide a highly structured framework for the delivery of corrective discipline, and they are especially useful for High Misbehavers. As is the case with Strikes, Charts is actually another variation on Tickets, the primary advantages being:

1. Tickets (or Strikes) is limited to use on a one-day-at-a-time basis only, but one chart can be used for up to a week (not always immediately, but eventually).
2. Children "graduate" through chart levels, thus providing them with a concrete means of seeing their own progress.

In addition to providing children with a good deal of clarity and certainty, the Charts system is also conducive to helping parents learn to be consistent in their enforcement of rules and expectations. I don't usually recommend the use of Charts earlier than the fourth birthday, but older three-year-olds are capable of catching on, given meticulous consistency on the part of their parents.

Daily Charts

Charts can be applied on a daily or weekly basis with children ages three through seven (up to the eighth birthday, I generally recommend that parents begin with six-block daily charts). While I don't advise starting Daily Charts with less than six blocks, I have had parents of some especially High Misbehavers start with as many as ten blocks. In any case, it's important that the child begin with a suitable margin of error. Nothing dooms a program like this to failure more than creating a "no-win" situation for the child. Too many blocks per day are equally counterproductive, however. In that case, the child isn't likely to take the program seriously. Daily charts are easiest to administer if one week's worth of charts is put on a single sheet of paper, as shown on the following pages. As with both Tickets and Strikes, the program requires a clearly defined list of target misbehaviors.

To demonstrate Daily Charts in use, we'll follow the story of Charlie, a four-year-old HM who has learned how to keep his parents in a near-constant state of wit's end. Because of his age, Charlie's Target Misbehavior List is initially limited to three prominent misbehaviors. For the time being, his parents are simply going to ignore, as well as they possibly can, misbehaviors that aren't on Charlie's list. If they can't ignore a certain behavior, then they're just going to have to deal with it as well as possible. Keep in mind that as a child brings misbehavior under control, even misbehaviors that weren't initially targeted begin to improve. If Charlie does something especially bad that isn't on his list, his parents are fully within their rights to override the program. If, for example, he spits out his food during dinner on Thursday, his parents can (and probably should) suspend the program for the remainder of the week and confine him to his room during that entire time. (A few days of room confinement, assuming the room is comfortable, is not going to scar a four-year-old's psyche.) As Charlie begins to master the program, his parents can add new targets to the list, but not more than one at a time.

Charlie's Target Misbehaviors

1. Refusing to do what we tell you to do.
2. Yelling at us.
3. Chasing the cat around the house.

Charlie's parents begin with six-block Daily Charts, shown below. Note that privileges are inserted in blocks 3, 2, and 1. (For a child who cannot yet read, consider using simple "icons" to represent privileges: for example, a swingset can represent going out to play.) Both the Daily Charts and the Target Misbehavior List are magnetized to the refrigerator. A set of Daily Charts covers Monday through Sunday. At the end of a seven-day chart period—after Charlie has gone to bed on Sunday evening—his parents take down that week's charts and put up a new, clean set so that it's already in place when Charlie arises on Monday morning.

Charlie's Daily Chart

	6	5	4	3	2	1
Monday				Outside	Friends/ TV	Room/ Bed
Tuesday				Outside	Friends/ TV	Room/ Bed
Wednesday				Outside	Friends/ TV	Room/ Bed
Thursday				Outside	Friends/ TV	Room/ Bed
Friday				Outside	Friends/ TV	Room/ Bed
Saturday				Outside	Friends/ TV	Room/ Bed
Sunday				Outside	Friends/ TV	Room/ Bed

The Procedure: On any given day, every time Charlie produces a target misbehavior, the parent who is closest to the scene of the crime simply:

1. Calls the misbehavior, as in "Chasing Blossom around the house is on your list, Charlie, and means you're losing a block [or number]."
2. Walks calmly to the refrigerator and crosses off the highest remaining on that day's chart, beginning (in this case) with block 6.
3. Directs Charlie to the "Thinking Chair" for a ten-minute time-out. (Charlie's parents have decided to impose a time-out every time a target misbehavior occurs, but this is optional. He is, however, given the choice of not sitting, in which case he simply loses the next block.)

With a six-block chart, the first three blocks are "free"—they constitute Charlie's daily margin of error. When Charlie loses block number 3, however, he loses the associated privilege associated with that block—in Charlie's chart, that's going outside to play—*for the remainder of the day*. He can still have friends over. He can still watch television or play his video game. He is still free to move about the entire house. When Charlie loses the next block, block 2, he loses both the privilege of having friends over for the remainder of that day and the privilege of television/electronics. When he loses block 1, he is confined to his room *for the remainder of the day* (except for the need to use the bathroom, chores, family meals, and accompanying his parents when they leave the house), and his bedtime is moved up at least one hour. Privileges are ordered such that the first privilege lost is that which allows Charlie the greatest degree of freedom. From there, each privilege lost further restricts his freedom until he is in his room awaiting early bedtime.

At the end of a seven-day chart period—Charlie's bedtime on Sunday evening—his parents take down that week's charts and put up a new, clean set so that it's in place when he arises on Monday morning. It's important that when Charlie's first misbehavior occurs on Monday, his parents do not have to scramble around for a new chart.

Most children master a six-block Daily Chart in two or three weeks. Mastery is achieved when your child loses no more than three or four privileges over a seven-day period. Once your child has cleared this hurdle, you "graduate" him to a five-block chart, thus reducing his margin of error from three blocks to two blocks. Or you can keep working with a six-block chart and add a misbehavior to the Target Misbehavior List. "Upping the ante" in one of these two fashions (but not both at the same time!) increases pressure on your child to continue improving self-control.

When your child masters a five-block chart, he graduates to a four-block chart, in which case his margin of error is one block per day (block 4). When he masters a four-block chart, he graduates to a three-block chart. But read carefully: *a child should never have less than a one-block daily margin of error.* So when your child graduates to a three-block Daily Chart, you move the privilege that was in block 3 to block 2, making block 3 a free block. In that case, once Charlie graduates to a three-block chart, the loss of block 2 means the loss of playing outside, having friends over, and television/electronics for the remainder of the day in question. The sequence is shown below.

Charlie's Daily Chart (Five Blocks)

	5	4	3	2	1
Monday			Outside	Friends/TV	Room/Bed
Tuesday			Outside	Friends/TV	Room/Bed
Wednesday			Outside	Friends/TV	Room/Bed
Thursday			Outside	Friends/TV	Room/Bed
Friday			Outside	Friends/TV	Room/Bed
Saturday			Outside	Friends/TV	Room/Bed
Sunday			Outside	Friends/TV	Room/Bed

Charlie's Daily Chart (Four Blocks)

	4	3	2	1
Monday		Outside	Friends/TV	Room/Bed
Tuesday		Outside	Friends/TV	Room/Bed
Wednesday		Outside	Friends/TV	Room/Bed
Thursday		Outside	Friends/TV	Room/Bed
Friday		Outside	Friends/TV	Room/Bed
Saturday		Outside	Friends/TV	Room/Bed
Sunday		Outside	Friends/TV	Room/Bed

Charlie's Daily Chart (Three Blocks)

	3	2	1
Monday		Outside/Friends/TV	Room/Bed
Tuesday		Outside/Friends/TV	Room/Bed
Wednesday		Outside/Friends/TV	Room/Bed
Thursday		Outside/Friends/TV	Room/Bed
Friday		Outside/Friends/TV	Room/Bed
Saturday		Outside/Friends/TV	Room/Bed
Sunday		Outside/Friends/TV	Room/Bed

It may take six to twelve weeks for a child to progress from a six- to a three-block chart. Be patient! Hang in there! Keep the faith! Stay the course! Never give up! Never surrender! Once your child masters a three-block Daily Chart, you have several options:

1. Discontinue the program. You have no more Target Misbehaviors to add, and the program has served its purpose—your child has learned good self-control.

2. Up the ante. Add a misbehavior to the Target Misbehavior List. This assumes that not all of your child's misbehaviors were included on the original list (because of his age, or because new ones have cropped up).

3. Graduate your child to Weekly Charts. When your child masters a three-block chart, *and your child is six or older*, you can transition to Weekly Charts. Don't do this, however, if your child's behavior is fine at this point. I see there are some folks who have questions. Yes?

Q & A

Q: **John, just to clarify: if my five-year-old loses all of his blocks on his Daily Chart and is confined to his room for the rest of the day, he can still come out of his room to use the bathroom, do chores, eat meals with the family, and go places with us when leaving him home isn't possible, right?**

A: Yes, that's right. He is still treated as a member of the family. He's isolated, not ostracized.

Q: **So what if he's out of his room for one of those reasons and he misbehaves? Do I start taking blocks from the next day's chart?**

A: Absolutely not. If misbehavior occurs after the loss of the last number on the chart, whether it's a Daily Chart or a Weekly Chart, you just have to respond as well as you can. Levying additional punishments violates the contract. No discipline plan is foolproof. They all have drawbacks, loopholes, and this is one of them. When you hit a snag like this, you just have to muddle through it as well as you can.

Q: **What if my child is on Daily Charts and he does something**

really bad that's not on his Target Misbehavior List?

A: You can cross off all of his remaining blocks for that day and send him directly to his room. You can override the program for more than one day if you feel that the misbehavior warrants it. You're not locked into the program, but don't let your frustration drive you to start crossing off blocks like you're having a manic episode. When it's time to "up the ante" on your child, add that misbehavior to the list.

Q: **Can certain behaviors result in the loss of more than one block?**

A: Yes, as long as that's specified in advance. Obviously, your child hitting you, spitting on you, or using foul language is a more serious offense than if he simply ignores an instruction from you or dawdles while doing something you've told him to do. You can, and probably should, assign different values, from one to three, for different misbehaviors. For example, using foul language can result in the loss of three blocks; calling you "dummy," two blocks; any other misbehavior, one block. You should also make it clear at the outset that any attempt to hit you, whether it connects or not, results in the loss of all blocks remaining on the Daily Chart or Weekly Chart at a minimum.

Q: **Once blocks are lost, can my child earn them back with good behavior or by doing extra chores around the house?**

A: No. You do not want to get involved in negotiations of that sort with your child. When parents negotiate such things with a child, they unwittingly undermine their own authority. A block lost is a block lost, period.

Weekly Charts

For children ages eight and older but younger than thirteen, I generally recommend starting with Weekly Charts. In most cases, a twelve-block chart is an appropriate beginning level, with at least eight free blocks. Under no circumstances should a child begin the program with less than ten blocks, where at least six are free. Weekly Charts are administered in the same way as are Daily Charts, the difference being that a weekly chart, as the name indicates, covers a seven-day period—Monday through Sunday. Like Daily Charts, a Weekly Chart works in conjunction with a Target Misbehavior List that initially contains no more than five specifically defined misbehaviors. When a target misbehavior occurs, remove the highest remaining block on that week's chart. Unlike Daily Charts, however, when your child begins to lose blocks associated with privileges, those privileges are lost *for the remainder of the week*.

CAUTION! Some Really-Really High Misbehavers will lose all of the blocks on a twelve-block Weekly Chart on day one, perhaps even within several hours. These volatile, defiant kids create a no-win situation for themselves right out of the gate. If you anticipate this problem with your child, then begin your child's (and your own) disciplinary rehabilitation with Daily Charts, even though he is eight or older. Start with a six-block Daily Chart. Graduate your child through the Daily Chart sequence as described previously. When your child has mastered a three-block Daily Chart, graduate him to a twelve-block Weekly Chart and go from there as described below.

Charlie's Weekly Chart (Twelve Blocks)

12	11	10	9
8	7	6	5
4 Bike/Play Outside	3 Having Friends Over	2 TV/Electronics	1 Room/Bed

With a Weekly Chart, mastery is defined thus: in a week's time, the child loses no privileges *for any significant period of time*. Let's say your child is on a twelve-block chart and loses only blocks 12 through 5 from the start of the Weekly Chart on Monday morning until Sunday at noon. Thus far, he's lost no privileges. Good for him! But suddenly the tide turns: he then proceeds to lose blocks 4, 3, 2, and 1, along with the associated privileges, between noon and bedtime on Sunday. Even though he had a bad last day, he has mastered a twelve-block chart. He did lose privileges, he but did not lose any of them for *a significant period of time.*

Once you've reached this point with your child, your child graduates from a twelve-block chart to a ten-block chart. When mastery occurs with ten blocks, you graduate your child to an eight-block chart, then a six-block chart. (The full sequence is shown below.) I do not recommend going below a six-block weekly chart. I also do not recommend a margin of error of less than three blocks on a Weekly Chart, in which case a six-block Weekly Chart would have privileges in blocks 3, 2, and 1. Note in the examples below, that as the overall size of the Weekly Chart is reduced, privileges are combined so that the loss of a block may mean the loss of more than one privilege for the remainder of the week.

Charlie's Weekly Chart (Ten Blocks)

10	9	8	7	6
5 Bike	4 Outside Play	3 Friends Over	2 TV	1 Room/Bed

Charlie's Weekly Chart (Eight Blocks)

8	7	6	5
4 Bike /Outside	3 Friends	2 TV	1 Room/Bed

Charlie's Weekly Chart (Six Blocks)

6	5	4
3 Bike /Outside	2 Friends /TV	1 Room/Bed

In most cases, mastery of a six-block Weekly Chart means that the program has served its purpose. If that's not good enough news, read this: my general finding has been that even when the original Target Misbehavior List does not include all outstanding misbehaviors, this process allows your child to develop enough self-control that even those misbehaviors not originally targeted begin to fade away. If, however, mastery of a six-block Weekly Chart has taken place but additional misbehaviors still remain, they can be added to the Target Misbehavior List without adding blocks to the Weekly Chart. Add them one at a time, however, and don't add another until the child has again attained mastery. Some folks have questions. Yes?

Q & A

Q: My child is pretty much a homebody. He usually prefers to stay at home, doesn't participate in after-school activities, and only has one friend. He likes being in his room and will stay there all day if I let him. I'm having a difficult time identifying more than a couple of privileges that would be meaningful to him. Will charts still work?

A: Charts are most effective if they incorporate at least three meaningful privileges, but if you can't identify more than two, then two it is. In that event, I'd begin the program with fewer blocks. For example, I'd begin him on a ten-block Weekly Chart in which eight blocks would be free. Most kids, no matter how self-limited their privileges, do not want to go to bed early, so that's always a good privilege to associate with the loss of block number 1.

Q: What is the upper age limit for Weekly Charts?

A: I do not usually recommend that children above age twelve be put on charts, but I have made *rare* exceptions with kids as old as fourteen. If you'd like my advice on disciplining teens, see my book *Teen-Proofing*.

Q: Can Daily or Weekly Charts be adapted to deal with behavior problems that are occurring at both home and school?

A: That's where I'm going next. Read on!

DAILY AND WEEKLY REPORT CARDS (FOR SCHOOL PROBLEMS)

Daily and Weekly Report Cards are a variation on Daily and Weekly Charts, the difference being that they target school misbehavior and performance. Daily Report Cards are generally suitable for children in kindergarten through grade six, but administration becomes difficult when the problem or problems in question occur in more than one teacher's class. In that event, Weekly Report Cards are the way to go. Weekly Reports can be used through high school. Regardless, both Daily and Weekly Report Cards can be configured to address either classroom behavior problems or underachievement, or both.

Daily Report Cards for Classroom Misbehavior

When classroom behavior is the issue, a Daily Report Card is really nothing more than a Daily Chart on an index card or half sheet of paper.

Before starting the program, it's necessary for the child's parents and teacher to collaborate on developing a Target Misbehavior List that specifically defines three to five outstanding classroom misbehaviors. I'm going to illustrate how Daily Report Cards work by relating the true story of Richie, who was in the third grade when his parents sought my help.

Richie's classroom behavior had been a problem since kindergarten and was getting worse as time went along. By the third grade, the school was suggesting that Richie had both attention-deficit hyperactivity disorder and oppositional defiant disorder. The school counselor was suggesting that Richie might respond well to certain drugs. But it was also obvious, from talking with both his teacher and his parents, that he was capable of exercising excellent self-control when he thought it would be to his advantage. Brain-based biological disorders do not wax and wane with offers of rewards or threats of punishment, so I knew there was nothing "wrong" with Richie. He had simply discovered, early on, the perverse pleasures of causing adults to become exasperated, and he luxuriated in the attention he received as a consequence, however negative it might have been.

First, I helped his teacher and parents develop a list of five target behaviors. If every one of Richie's misbehaviors had been listed, the Target Misbehavior List would have been more than twenty items long. That would have created an administrative nightmare; so, fairly confident that when a few misbehaviors were under control, the rest would follow suit, we started with only five. When finished, the Target Misbehavior List looked like this:

Richie's Target Misbehaviors

1. Talking without permission
2. Not paying attention
3. Making fun of other children
4. Leaving your desk without permission
5. Refusing to obey Mrs. Wilson

Next, we developed a six-block Daily Report Card that looked as shown below (six blocks is generally where I recommend starting). Note that the privileges listed in blocks 3, 2, and 1 are at-home privileges. In other words, as those blocks are lost at school, privileges are lost at home. This builds a "Bridge of Communication and Consequences" between school and home, ensuring that the child's parents and teacher are on the same page and that the child is held reliably accountable for misbehavior.

Richie's Daily Report Card		Date: _____
6	5	4
3 Outside	2 Electronics	1 Room/Bed

Teacher's Signature: _____   (Put Comments on Back)

The Procedure: At the outset of the program, Richie was given a folder of Daily Report Cards to keep in his desk. The folder also contained the Target Misbehavior List. When he arrived at school in the morning, Richie's first responsibility was to put a Daily Report Card on his teacher's desk. His teacher, Mrs. Wilson, kept a copy of Richie's Target Misbehavior List in her desk. Every time Richie produced a target misbehavior, Mrs. Wilson calmly reprimanded him (e.g., "Richie, you're out of your desk without permission. Please get back in your seat. That's a number."), walked to her desk, and crossed off the highest remaining number on his Daily Report Card.

Richie's first three blocks—6, 5, and 4—were "free" (margin of error), but only in the sense that Richie lost no at-home privileges when he lost those blocks. The consequences Richie experienced at home supplemented, but did not replace, classroom consequences. So if Richie misbehaved in class and a consequence—being denied recess, for example—was appropriate and called for, Richie experienced that as well.

If possible (and sometimes it is not), the program can be designed such that the child loses specified privileges both at home and at school simultaneously. That simply requires that some or all of blocks 3, 2, and 1 contain both at-school and at-home privileges. The former are written in one color, the latter in another. Example: When the child loses block 3, he loses the at-home privilege of being able to go outside and play and the at-school privilege of being able to go to the computer station if he's completed his work. When he child loses block 2, he loses television privileges at home and recess at school, but *only if recess has not yet occurred*. If it has already taken place, then only the at-home privilege is lost. Losing block 1 means the child is confined to his room after school and goes to bed early and must sit out the thirty-minute free-play period at the end of the school day. If it seems complicated to set the program up that way, don't.

Back to Richie: At the end of the school day, it was Richie's responsibility to ask Mrs. Wilson for the Daily Report Card. She signed it, put any comments she wanted to make on the back, and gave it to Richie to take home. At this point in the program, two possibilities arise:

1. *The child forgets to ask his teacher for the Daily Report Card at the end of the day.* In that event, the teacher does not remind the child or chase him down. When the child arrives home without the Daily Report Card, no excuses are accepted, and all privileges are automatically lost.
2. *The child remembers to ask his teacher for the Daily Report Card but loses it on the way home from school.* Again, no excuses are accepted, and all privileges are automatically lost. The child's parents do not call the school to ask the teacher how many blocks were lost.

This puts responsibility for building the aforementioned Bridge of Communication and Consequences squarely on the child's shoulders. Most children forget to ask the teacher for the Daily Report Card once or twice, do without privileges at home as a consequence, and stop forgetting. It's amazing how quickly "forgetfulness" can be cured by simply assigning a child full responsibility for its consequences.

Richie's problems in school mirrored similar problems at home. Everyone agreed it would be in his best interest if both sets of problems were addressed simultaneously. So when Richie got home, his mother noted what privileges had already been lost and magnetized the Daily Report Card to the refrigerator alongside an at-home Target Misbehavior

List that basically addressed Richie's habit of ignoring and defying instructions from his parents. His parents then picked up where Mrs. Wilson had left off. Let's say, for example, that Richie lost blocks 6 through 3 at school, meaning that he came home having already lost the privilege associated with block 3 (playing outside). At home, he loses block 2 at six o'clock, which means he cannot watch television or indulge in any electronics from that point on. He loses block 1 at six thirty, so he goes to his room for the remainder of the day and goes to bed early.

Q & A

Q: Say the child comes home having lost the privilege of being able to play outside, but for some reason—perhaps it's raining—outside play isn't possible. Does the child lose some other privilege instead?

A: No. If a lost privilege is "neutralized" for any reason, no other privileges are substituted.

Q: What happens on non-school days?

A: On weekends and other non-school days, the Daily Report Card becomes a Daily Chart. It's put up on the refrigerator first thing in the morning, and you cross off blocks for misbehaviors that are enumerated on the at-home Target Misbehavior List.

Q: Can a Daily Report Card be used when my child changes classes and has more than one teacher in the course of a school day?

A: Daily Reports are easiest to administer when only one teacher is involved. If the child is a problem in several classes, with several teachers, I often recommend limiting the program to only the teacher with whom the child spends the greatest amount of time during the school day. My consistent finding is that as a child's behavior improves with one teacher, it improves with every teacher. However, when multiple teachers are involved, and depending on the nature and severity of the problem, Weekly Report Cards may be the way to go.

Q: **My child's classroom behavior is fine. The problem is that she doesn't complete work on time and when she does, it's often very sloppily done. We know she can do better because whenever we offer her a reward, she shapes up. Then, when she gets the reward, it's back to square one. Can Daily Report Cards be used in a situation of that sort?**

A: Absolutely, but instead of a chart, the Daily Report Card would contain a Statement of Achievement that the teacher would sign off on at the end of the school day. If the teacher signs the statement, the child has access to all after-school privileges. If the teacher does not sign the statement (puts an X in the signature space), all privileges are lost. If, say, two teachers are involved, then each teacher's signature is worth a certain block of privileges. A sample Statement of Achievement looks like this:

Molly's Daily Report Card

Date: _____

Statement of Achievement: Today, Molly completed all of her work, and all work was satisfactory.

Signed: _____
(Please write any comments on the back.)

Weekly Report Cards for Classroom Misbehavior

Weekly Report Cards are my usual approach of choice when a child changes teachers throughout the day and the problem, whether misbehavior or underachievement, occurs in more than one teacher's class. As the name indicates, a Weekly Report Card covers a week's worth of school behavior or performance. Here is a sample Weekly Report Card, where the problem is underachievement:

Rambo's Weekly Report

For Week Ending: _____

Statement of Achievement: This week, Rambo completed all of his work, turned it in on time, and all of his work was satisfactory (C or better). Please circle either Yes or No and sign your name. Thank you for helping Rambo be a good student! (Please put any comments on the back.)

Mrs. Willis: _____	Yes	No
Mr. Davis: _____	Yes	No
Mr. Elton: _____	Yes	No
Mrs. Phipps: _____	Yes	No

The Statement of Achievement is the "centerpiece" of the Weekly Report Card. It can, as in the example above, target underachievement, or it can target misbehavior. When a child is both a behavior problem and an underachiever, I do *not* recommend targeting both problems at once. In those cases, my usual finding has been that by targeting only underachievement, misbehavior will greatly improve as the child's school performance comes up to par.

On the last day of the school week (Friday, usually), the youngster takes the Weekly Report to each of his teachers. Each teacher circles either Yes or No based on whether or not the child's work for the week is up to par as described by the Statement of Achievement, and then signs the card. The child must obtain a Yes rating from all teachers involved in the program in order to enjoy all privileges from that Friday afternoon to the next Friday afternoon. Failure to obtain one Yes results in the loss of one privilege, like watching television through the following Friday. Failure to obtain two Yeses results in the loss of *all* privileges for the next seven days.

Q & A

Q. This seems like a plan that might work with my son, who's a sophomore in high school. What do you think?

A: Weekly Reports, unlike the other plans set forth in this chapter, do work with kids older than twelve. I've used them for kids up through high school, in fact.

Q: I hate to think this about my child, but I think he might get his friends to sign his Weekly Report Cards. What can I do to prevent this?

A. If you think your child might forge his teachers' signatures, then you should obtain, in person, a sample of each signature before starting the program.

Q. My child's science teacher is complaining that this is too much work for her. Do I abandon the entire program since she won't participate?

A. Obviously, as is the case with Daily Report Cards, you'll have to obtain each teacher's commitment to the program before it starts. If a teacher says she's too busy or for any other reason doesn't want to participate in the program, then don't fight city hall. Just leave her off the report.

Q. My daughter tells me her teacher left school early and she wasn't able to get her signature. What should I do?

A. If your child comes home without a certain teacher's rating and signature and complains that she couldn't find the teacher after school, then simply tell her that if she gets the signature and rating on Monday, the withheld privilege will be restored for the remainder of the week (assuming the rating is Yes).

KICKED OUT OF THE GARDEN

Occasionally a behavior problem is so *big* that nothing short of what I call "nuclear discipline" will do. Your great-grandparents called it "lowering the boom." Regardless of terminology, the discipline in question causes shock-and-awe. What I call "kicking a child out of the Garden of Eden" is a variation on this theme. I reserve it for only two situations: an individual problem that has grown to *huge* proportion, or a *huge* cluster of problems. The Garden of Eden is the child's room, which for most of today's kids is a veritable paradise of toys and games and electronic equipment—a self-contained entertainment complex!

Kicking a child out of the Garden (we'll call it "Kicking" for short) means:

- The child's room is stripped of anything and everything that is nonessential, leaving only a bed, chest of drawers, desk, lamp, school supplies, and *essential* clothing, taking those clothes that are mere adornments.
- The child is withdrawn from all after-school activities.
- All nonessential purchases are put on hold.
- All privileges are cancelled indefinitely.

The result is as close as one can get to a military school environment without actually sending the child to one. To avoid a potential all-out battle (and almost certainly a highly emotional scene), I recommend transforming the child's room into a military school dorm room when the child is not at home. Put the things taken from the room where he cannot possibly gain access to them, even if that means a rented storage locker.

Once the room is emptied out, a Target Misbehavior List is posted on the refrigerator. Remember, it might only contain one *big* misbehavior, like "Cursing." When he arrives home, the child is told he will get his things back after no target misbehaviors (or *the* target misbehavior) have occurred for a certain period of time.

How long? Fourteen days is the minimum length of time. Remember, the targeted behavior or behaviors are *huge*. It may take the child six weeks to go fourteen straight days without a target. In certain cases, however, I have recommended that a child go up to a full month without a target—especially if there's only one target, like cursing—before getting his Garden back. The length of the "kick" is a judgment call, but parents can create a no-win situation by combining a lengthy Target Misbehavior List with the requirement that the child be problem-free for, say, forty days and forty nights. Better to target one to three "biggies" and keep the requirement to fourteen days.

A fourteen-day (or thirty-day) chart, as shown below, is posted alongside the Target Misbehavior List. Every day that no target misbehavior occurs, the child receives a star or happy face in one of the blocks on the chart. If a target misbehavior occurs before the required number of stars is earned, the chart is taken down, a new one is put up, and the required period begins anew.

Kicking Out of the Garden Chart

14	13	12	11	10	9	8
7	6	5	4	3	2	1

I have found Kicking to be very effective when dealing with especially horrendous behaviors like throwing wild tantrums, beligerent disobedience and/or disrespect, hitting other family members, and cursing. Sometimes, even when your child's misbehaviors are legion, I recommend targeting only the *biggest* misbehavior while ejecting your child from the Garden. When your child has earned his things back, target the remaining misbehaviors with either Tickets or Daily Charts.

Whereas most of the discipline approaches described in this chapter are optimal for kids three through twelve, Kicking has been successful with teenagers. In order to work, it definitely needs to be customized to your child's developmental age. Here are some real-life examples to help you see what Kicking might look like with preschoolers, school-age children, and teens.

Kicking a Preschooler Out of the Garden

Georgia was four when her parents asked for my help with her behavior. She was a cute little thing who could become a three-foot-tall tyrant at a moment's notice. Her parents had made the mistake of catering to her—giving her just about everything she wanted, when she wanted it—since she was a toddler. As a consequence, Georgia was demanding, ungrateful, disrespectful, disobedient, and had mastered the art of throwing monumental tantrums whenever her parents did not obey her or failed to obey quickly enough.

I discussed the option of Kicking with her parents and they agreed that nothing short of "the boom" would stop Georgia's downhill slide. We decided to target only three of her many misbehaviors: sticking out her tongue at her parents, calling them names like "stupid" and "dummy," and throwing tantrums (crying, screaming, falling on the floor, thrashing about, throwing things, kicking things . . . you name it). After sending her to her grandparents' house one Saturday (the grands were only too happy to cooperate), Georgia's parents sterilized her room, reducing it to bare essentials. They put the Target Misbehavior List up on the refrigerator along with a thirty-block chart. They rejected the option of a lesser chart, expressing their conviction that Georgia was capable of controlling herself when she wanted to. I was dubious, but they felt that expecting her to keep her tongue in her mouth, her rude comments to herself, and her tantrums bottled up inside of her for thirty days straight was not unreasonable.

When Georgia came home from the grandparents' house, her parents showed her her "new" room and explained the program to her. She stuck out her tongue, called them "stupid," and threw the Mother of All Tantrums. It lasted two hours during which she acted and sounded like she was possessed by demons. Finally, she stopped screaming and tried another tack: sobbing pitifully. For the next couple of hours, she sobbed and begged and promised to be good and then, when her parents held firm, she threw another tantrum.

The next few months were not easy for Georgia. She would make some progress, then have a relapse; then make some progress, and then have another relapse. It was definitely a two-steps-forward, one-step-back process. After three months, she made her goal.

Shortly thereafter, her parents brought Georgia to my office for a checkup. I asked her how she was doing.

"I'm happy!" she said, with a great big smile.

I saw tears in her parents' eyes. In fact, there were tears in mine.

Kicking a Grade Schooler Out of the Garden: Part One

I recommended this approach to the parents of a nine-year-old girl—I'll call her Lorna—who was not completing fourth-grade classwork, not doing homework, not studying for tests, and in danger of failing a number of subjects. The problem had started early in the third grade and had gotten progressively worse since. Lorna's teacher and the counselor at school were convinced that the girl had ADHD and had been petitioning the parents to get her tested and put on medication.

Instead, her parents kicked her out of the Garden in November. Within a month, Lorna had managed to cure herself of a genetically transmitted, biochemical imbalance (my tongue is in my cheek, folks). Here are the mother's own words:

> It was the hardest thing I've ever done, but it was the best. We were headed into the third straight year of Lorna failing to complete classwork, and a school was determined to label her ADD and constantly dragging me into inquisitions where I was forced to defend our decision not to medicate.
>
> Up until kicking her out of the Garden, we had tried everything. I monitored her homework, making sure it was done. We took her to tutors. We took away daily and weekend privileges (but nothing, I later realized, of any real consequence).
>
> When we finally made our daughter see that her irresponsible

behavior would result in big-time consequences and that she would have to earn back her toys and privileges, she finally realized we were serious.

Lorna immediately began doing her work, studying, and making decent grades. We gave back her privileges and possessions just before Christmas, with the understanding that the next time she required being kicked out of the Garden the kicking was going to last for a minimum of two months. It's now March and she's only failed to complete her work one day since we began in November. We disciplined strongly for that, and it's not happened again. She finishes her work, her teacher is ecstatic, the ADHD-Alert file kept by the counselor was closed in December, and her grade in every subject is now satisfactory.

The best news of all: She's a much, much happier child. And we are much, much happier parents!

Lorna's success story just proves that stubborn misbehavior requires stubborn discipline and stubborn love. The next story is further proof.

Kicking a Grade Schooler Out of the Garden: Part Two

Bosco was an eight-year-old whose parents described him as a "poor sport." He had been asked to leave several sports programs because of rudeness to other players and disrespect to adults, but every time they put him in an after-school sport, the rudeness and disrespect began anew. The parents had tried various punishments. None had worked.

Bosco's mother was the only parent at the first appointment with me. She said, "I think he's just not as sports-minded as his dad wants him to be."

I was about to give that some credence when she added, "His teachers report that he is a bad sport if he can't be first to do whatever the class is doing. And when other children make mistakes in class, he makes fun of them."

Aha! Obviously, this was not a matter of being a "poor sport" who was rebelling against pressure from Dad to excel at athletics. Bosco's behavior was a problem when a sport wasn't the issue. This mom, these parents, needed to get their heads out of the sand. I told the mother to bring her husband to the next appointment. He came, reluctantly. After all, he had every reason to believe I was going to blame him for the problem. Instead, I told them that Bosco was exhibiting some very pronounced antisocial behaviors that were likely to worsen over time. Children who are verbal bullies at age eight are likely to be physical bullies in their early teens. The antisocial child is nearly always described, by the way, as not caring what consequences ensue as a result of his or her behavior.

I asked lots of questions about their marriage, their other two children, their family life, and came to the conclusion that Bosco's problems were of his own making. It's often, but not always, the case that children who frequently engage in antisocial behavior of this sort come from families where there is a high level of marital discord and dysfunction. This didn't apply here. If it had, I'd have recommended marriage therapy. Since that wasn't needed, I told the parents Bosco needed a *huge* wake-up call and recommended that they kick him out of the Garden.

The next day, Bosco came home from school to find that his room had been "sterilized." All of his possessions, save furniture and *essential* clothing, had been removed and transferred to a rented storage unit.

With my help, the parents had drawn up a comprehensive list of "misfit" behaviors and gave Bosco a copy. The list included making fun of or laughing at other children, being rude to other children or adults, making verbal threats to other children, disrespecting adults, becoming angry if he wasn't first in line, and so on.

Next, the parents made Bosco write a one-page letter of apology to his class and to the baseball team he was currently a member of. He had to rewrite the letters until they approved of them, at which point he had to read them out loud to the class and the team.

From that point on, Bosco's parents met with the teacher every week to get a progress report. Every Friday evening, they held a home conference with Bosco at which his progress, or lack of it, was reviewed. He was kicked out of the Garden for a minimum of one month, during which time an incident at school or during baseball restarted the month. In addition, any incident would require a letter of apology to the person or persons he had disrespected. After a full month of no incidents—a full month of good behavior at school, baseball, and home—his parents were to begin restoring his privileges and possessions, one thing at a time.

It took four months for Bosco to make the mark. At that point, I told the parents that although their son had finally found the right track, his rehabilitation was probably not complete. There would be future incidents, I warned, and told them that when a relapse occurred, they had to start over: they had to put him out of the Garden for a minimum of a month, have him write a letter of apology, and start the weekly teacher conferences. In other words, this was likely to be a long haul, but the good news was that he was now on the right track, headed in the right direction.

Kicking a Teenager Out of the Garden

I have recommended that teens be kicked out of the Garden, but the decision to do so with a child over thirteen must be made prudently. If you're having major problems with a teen, I recommend that before you decide to do something along these lines, you read my book *Teen-Proofing*.

Sometimes, instead of sterilizing the teenager's room, I recommend taking away the one or two possessions that have assumed "idol" status in the teen's life: cell phone, car, computer, video game. Concerning the latter, I began to argue in the early 1980s that video games were addictive, and if the research to date is not completely clear on the subject, the anecdotal evidence is compelling, to say the least. More and more parents are refusing to allow their children access to these nefarious devices, but most of the stories that come my way involve children who are already addicted.

"What do we do now?" their parents ask, to which I advise the most effective, albeit painful, of all anti-addiction programs: cold turkey. Some parents don't have the gumption, or I must suppose so because I never hear from them again. But then there are the occasional stories of deliverance, such as the one shared by the mother of a seventeen-year-old "gamer."

"Surly, uncooperative, negative, and reclusive" was his parents' description of him. The problems had started shortly after getting a state-of-the-art video console for his thirteenth birthday and had worsened from there. At age seventeen, he rarely came out of his room when he was home. He even refused to eat most meals with the family. In addition, his parents were aware that he was up half the night and his grades were suffering as a consequence.

His parents said, "If he's not at school or work, he's on his computer or video game pretty much every waking moment." I told them they needed to take control where their son had lost control, but they ended up cutting him back to four hours a day on school days and eight hours a day on weekends. No, seriously. The mother later admitted, "I obviously am a total wimp" and "I feel really stupid about not having much backbone."

They contacted me again two months later to tell me that things had gone from bad to worse. Whenever one of them tried to enforce the limit, the boy exploded. He pounded furniture, yelled, called his parents names, accused them of being controlling, and maintained that it was his computer and they had no right to limit his playing time. That describes addictive behavior. His mom was in a lot of pain, I could tell. She implored me to give her the strength to take the computer away from him, saying she didn't know if she could take the ensuing meltdown.

I pointed out that as his parents, they had a responsibility to do what was best for him, whether he liked what they did or not. They wanted to wait until his grades came out to decide whether to take the computer away. I told them one cannot bargain with an addict and win. Take the computer away, I said, and do not ever give it back, even if he begins making straight A's.

A week or so later, they sent this e-mail: "We took his computer away. Wow, what a horrible scene. He went on and on, acting like the world was coming to an end, but we stuck to our guns and I feel like a miracle has occurred. The next day, he worked around the house all day and actually went out to dinner with us. The next day, he worked part of the day and was as pleasant and relaxed as can be for the rest of the evening. Today he got home from school and actually has a friend over. I need to tell you that when we were out to dinner two nights ago he said that although he was initially very angry at what we did, he actually felt kind of relieved. Isn't that wild? I know that there may be some rough patches ahead, but I feel like I have my son back."

Here come those tears again.

PILING ON

In football, "piling on" occurs when defensive players continue to fall on top of an offensive player after he's been tackled. Because it's unnecessary as well as dangerous, piling on is illegal—in football, that is.

In parenting it's perfectly legal, but then in parenting "piling on" does not refer to tackling a child and then falling on top of him and refusing to let him up! It refers to dispensing multiple consequences over a prolonged period of time for one offense. As such, the child is reminded of and punished for the offense over and over and over and maybe even over and over again. Piling On is very effective at establishing a permanent memory; therefore, it is a highly effective means of dealing with misbehavior—one of the most effective, in fact. But don't let yourself become carried away with it. Always keep in mind what I've said earlier and can't say often enough: the more you use one discipline method, the less effective, over time, it will become. Mix it up!

As you will see, Piling On should be reserved for relatively major offenses, but it can also be used, with discretion, for small misbehaviors you want to nip in the bud because you can foresee them growing into potentially huge issues in the future.

"Well, John," a reader asks, "since any small misbehavior has the potential of becoming big, aren't you saying Piling On can be used for just about anything?" Yes, it can be, but a lack of discretion is likely to result in overuse. Beyond that, all I can say is you're just going to have to use your common sense where Piling On is concerned (or any other strategy for that matter).

Let's say nine-year-old Juniper Swashbuckle, angry at his mother for refusing to let him ride his bike to the shopping center with a friend (whose mother has given permission), calls her a "jerk." Whoa! Because there's really no meaningful consequence she can levy on Juniper at that very moment, she takes a deep breath and says simply, "Well, isn't that interesting!" and continues to go about her business, even whistling a happy tune.

Two hours later, another of Juniper's friends comes over and asks if Juniper can come outside and toss a football back and forth.

"Can I, Mom?" he asks.

"No," she says. "Sorry."

"Why?" he asks, pointing out that he's done his chores.

"I guess I'm just a jerk, like you said," she says, and walks away.

Juniper follows her, assuring her that he's sorry and will never call her a jerk again. Really. It just slipped out. He didn't mean it.

"Good," his mom says, and goes about her business.

After a moment or two of confusion, Juniper asks, "So can I go out?"

"No."

"But Mom! I'm sorry! I promise I'll never call you a jerk again!"

"Promise?"

"Yes, Mom, I promise."

"Good. Are you sorry?"

"Yes, Mom, I'm sorry. Really."

"Thank you."

"So can I go out?"

"No."

"But why?"

"Because when you commit an offense against someone, an offense of disrespect, as you did to me when you called me a jerk, saying you're sorry isn't enough. It's fine, and it's the right thing to say if you're really and truly sorry and not just trying to get something, or get out of being punished, but it's not enough. When you commit an offense against someone, you have to pay a price. You have to suffer punishment. That's the way it is. So I appreciate that you're sorry, and I believe you are going to try not to ever again call me or anyone else a jerk, but you still have to be punished. So you can't go outside with Redbud, and that's that."

Two days later, on a Saturday, Juniper gets a phone call from a friend who asks if he wants to go with him and his mom to the afternoon movie.

Juniper goes to his mother and asks her permission. She says no.

"Why?"

"Because you called me a jerk two days ago, that's why."

"But you already punished me!" Juniper exclaims.

"Your punishment isn't over yet," Mom calmly explains.

"But this isn't fair!"

"If I was nine years old, I would think the same thing."

"I told you I was sorry!"

"And I thanked you."

"I told you I'd never do it again!"

"And I think that's great."

"Mom!"

"Juniper?"

"What?"

"You can stop now. You're not going to the movies."

The next day, Juniper asks if he and a friend can go fishing at the local pond after church.

"Sorry, no."

"Why?"

"Because you called me a jerk three days ago."

"Mom!"

"Juniper?"

"What?"

"You're not going fishing, and you're going to bed right after supper tonight."

"But I didn't do anything else!"

"I know, but I'm going to make sure you never forget calling me a jerk."

"But I told you I'm not going to call you that again!"

"Good." And she walks away.

Two days later, on Tuesday, Juniper reminds his mother that she has to take him to soccer practice.

"You're not going to soccer practice."

"Why?"

"You tell me."

"Are you kidding?" Juniper exclaims. "Is it because I called you a jerk last week?"

"Bingo."

"Mom! When are you going to stop punishing me for that?"

"When you stop acting like every time I punish you it's unfair. None of your punishments has hurt you as much as it hurt me when you called me a jerk. So, when you stop acting like being punished is unfair, I'll stop the punishments."

"Okay, Mom," Juniper says. "It's not unfair."

"That's better."

"So can I go to soccer?"

"Nope," she says.

"But if I don't go to practice, I can't play in the game tomorrow!"

"Is that unfair?"

Juniper barely stops himself from saying that yes, it's unfair. He thinks for a moment. Then, with great resignation, he says, "No, Mom, it's not unfair."

"You're getting there!" Mom says.

Two days later, after missing the soccer game, Juniper comes to his mom and asks if he can go outside and ride his bike around the neighborhood with a friend.

His mom fixes him in her gaze. She asks, "If I said no, would it be unfair?"

Juniper ponders that for a moment. Finally, he says, "No, it wouldn't be unfair. I would deserve it for calling you a jerk."

"Thank you. Yes, you can go bike riding with your friend."

Let me assure you, dear reader, Juniper Swashbuckle will never, ever call his mother a jerk again. In fact, he will never again call her by any inappropriate nomenclature. In fact, he will forever be extremely careful how he speaks to his mother, and his father, and later, his girlfriends, and later still, his wife.

Caution! Use Piling On sparingly, selectively, with great prudence. If you overuse it, it will lose its effectiveness and all you will accomplish is creating a very resentful and probably very rebellious child.

"THE DOCTOR" MAKES HOUSE CALLS

Shortly after I finished graduate school, a friend of mine shared with me a book on "Indirect Hypnosis," written by Milton Erickson, a most unorthodox psychiatrist if ever there was one.[3] "Indirect" meant that Erickson didn't use swinging watches or a soothing monotone voice to encourage his subject to go into a trance. In fact, Erickson rarely put anyone in a trance. Instead—and this is admittedly simplifying his methods—he simply suggested things to people while they were fully conscious. A lot of his work was done with children, and one of the things Erickson pointed out was that up to age nine or ten, children are very impressionable and therefore suggestible. That quality can be exploited by people with evil purposes, but it can also be used to help children get over certain "humps" in their lives.

Based on Erickson's work, I developed an approach to behavior problems with children that capitalizes on their suggestibility. I call it "The Doctor," and—this may sound self-promoting, but it's the truth—I've never had a parent tell me it failed. The Doctor is based on three unarguable facts:

1. No matter how stubbornly a child misbehaves, a behavior problem is a burden to a child. He would rather get rid of the problem and behave properly. He just doesn't know how. He's a child, after all.
2. A child with a behavior problem doesn't know how the problem started and can't explain why he has it. In other words, the child is as much in the dark about the problem as are his parents.
3. A child is more inclined to accept the authority of a third party (e.g., a doctor) than he is the authority of his parents, and this is

especially true of a child who has acquired or developed a behavior problem or problems.

Consistent with Erickson's findings, the Doctor does his best work with children below age ten. I've called him in on a broad range of problems, ranging from belligerent defiance to various fears. Here are several true stories from the Doctor's files.

The Doctor Cures Suppertime Anorexia!

Lucy refused to eat what her parents put on her plate at suppertime. The problem started when she was a toddler and became steadily worse. Every family supper turned into a drama, if not an out-and-out battle, as her parents tried to get Lucy to eat and she steadfastly refused. Her parents' feelings vacillated between anger, guilt, and worry. When they were angry, they insisted that she eat what everyone else was eating. When they felt guilty and anxious, they would fix a special meal for her and serve it with great obsequiousness.

Enter the Doctor! Lucy's parents sat her down one afternoon, after school, and told her that they had spoken to the Doctor about her refusal to eat what was put in front of her at suppertime.

With very serious expressions on their faces, they said something along these lines: "The Doctor told us that when children your age won't eat their supper, it's because they're overtired. It's because they haven't been getting enough sleep. Not getting enough sleep, the Doctor said, causes children to have bad reactions to food. So the Doctor says that when you refuse to eat or act like the food we have served you is bad, we have to put you to bed right away. More sleep will solve the problem. And honey, we're so sorry. We thought you were just being difficult about food. Now we know we just haven't been making sure you get enough sleep."

This is an explanation, however fictitious and ultimately absurd, that even a six-year-old can understand. Besides, a doctor said so! By age two, a child has figured out that that guy in the white coat called "the doctor" has almost magical authority. When he says, "Do this," people do it. By invoking the Doctor's authority, the power struggle that's developed over the problem—whatever it might be—between the parents and the child is effectively defused, nullified.

Engaging the Doctor in a power struggle is impossible, if not unthinkable, because he is not real. And by the way, since inventing the Doctor was clearly in Lucy's best interest, this does not qualify as a lie. This was helpful, not hurtful. It was no more of a "lie" than telling a child that the Tooth Fairy came in the middle of the night and left that dollar under the pillow. In Lucy's case, the explanation provided by the Doctor provided her with the means of gradually moving past this little glitch in her life. She really didn't want to be such a problem at the dinner table; she just didn't know how to stop. Add in the consequence of going to bed early and you have a little girl who finally had a plausible explanation of why she reacts negatively to food and finally found the motivation to do all she could to bring her "suppertime anorexia" under control as quickly as possible. And she did. In no time, Lucy was eating whatever her parents put on her plate at suppertime. Even broccoli.

From SAD to Glad in Two Days!

I was speaking at a church in Durham, North Carolina, one cold wintry evening. During a break in my seminar, a mother approached me and thanked me for referring her to the Doctor. Seems her five-year-old son, Frankie, had suffered since age two from a raging (literally) case of what mental health professionals call "separation anxiety."

Every time Mom took Frankie to his preschool program or left him with a sitter, Frankie had a major meltdown. I emphasize *major*. He would scream, cling, become hysterical, and generally act certifiable. Otherwise, mind you, Frankie was a normal kid in all respects. Oh, I should tell you: Frankie hates to take naps. I mean *hates*.

Shortly before his fifth birthday, Frankie's mom read a column of mine in which I described one of the Doctor's miracle cures. She decided to ask him to make a house call.

That afternoon, following one of Frankie's certifiable meltdowns over being taken to his preschool program, his mom sat him down and told him that she'd talked to a doctor about his little problem. The Doctor, she said, was concerned and told her that Frankie is throwing "don't leave me!" fits because he's not getting enough sleep.

"So," she said to Frankie, "on those days when you have a fit because I leave you at your program, you have to take a nap. Your doctor says so. He also says you have to take a nap the next day if you have a fit over being left with a sitter at night. And Frankie, since you had a fit this morning, you have to take a nap this afternoon, right now."

She promptly took Frankie to his room and put him to bed. After about forty-five minutes of howling, screaming, crying, and pleading, he fell asleep. The next day, when his mom took him to his preschool program, he got out of the car and walked right in, with nary a backward glance. And Frankie hasn't had a problem with separation since.

It's fair to say that if Frankie's mom had sought help from a mental health professional, there is considerable likelihood that Frankie would have been diagnosed with separation anxiety disorder (SAD). Said professional might well have taken Frankie into talk therapy or play therapy in order to help him work through the supposed "issues" that were causing the problem. It's anyone's guess as to how much time and money this process might have taken (not to mention the cost of continuing consultations with Frankie's parents). Furthermore, the therapy might not have resulted in progress (in fact, the problem might have grown worse in the meantime) in which case perhaps said therapist might have given Frankie yet another diagnosis and scheduled yet more treatment.

Frankie's story simply proves that there are times when common sense trumps graduate school.

I should mention that whereas the Doctor usually ties the problem, whatever it is, into a lack of sleep, he has also prescribed no television or video games (sometimes in combination with early bedtime) as cures for various behavior problems. The key to the success of one of the Doctor's prescriptions is that the child would rather have the "therapeutic" privilege or privileges than the behavior problem.

CHAPTER FOUR

The Top Seven Behavior Problems of All Time . . . Solved!

Now that you have the tools, the next step is to match problem with strategy. Toward that end, I've selected the Top Seven Behavior Problems of All Time-and-Eternity-Amen, and described, usually in anecdote form, how parents can pluck these vexing disciplinary thorns from their sides. The examples given in this chapter and the next will give you enough "ammunition" to solve even the thorniest of troublesome behaviors.

BEDTIME BATTLES (AND RELATED FEARS)

The most common bedtime battle involves children who will not go to bed and stay there. They get up numerous times, asking for another kiss, asking a question, wanting to tell their parents something, and so on. These kids can think of endless creative reasons to get out of bed and come out of their bedrooms, driving their parents slowly crazy in the process.

Robbie, age three, was one such child. During the day, he was obedient —unusually so, in fact. But he made up for his daytime cooperativeness in the evening. His parents would put him to bed, help him say his prayers, tuck him in, kiss him good night, and leave his room, wishing him a good night's sleep. As soon as they were downstairs, beginning to relax, Robbie would get up, walk down the stairs, and ask for something like another glass of water. They'd give him the water, take him back upstairs, put him in bed, etc., and he would appear in the living room within minutes, wanting to tell them something. He would keep this up until they went to bed. Most nights, they would go to bed long before they had intended to just to get Robbie to go to sleep.

They came to me hoping I could prevent Robbie from becoming an abused child. I recommended the same strategy that had worked with my daughter, Amy, when she was Robbie's age. When they put Robbie to bed, they hung a cheap but colorful necklace on his inner doorknob, where he could see it. The necklace on the doorknob meant he could get out of his bed. When he did, he had to take the necklace off the doorknob and bring it to his parents. Giving them the necklace meant he could ask a question, tell them something, get a glass of water, or whatever. Then they put him back in bed, but did not rehang the necklace on his doorknob. They kept it. If he got out of bed again, he would not be able to give his parents the necklace when he came downstairs. The penalty for that was twofold: first, he could not play with his favorite toy the next day, and second, he had to go to bed right after supper the next day. The next night, whether he went to bed early or not, his parents put him to bed, went through the bedtime ritual, then left his room, hanging the necklace on his doorknob, and the understanding was the same.

At first, and this was predictable, Robbie acted like he cared zero about the silly necklace. But after going without his favorite toy and having to go to bed early for four days, he began to show signs of improvement. Within a week, he was cured of chronic getoutofbeditis. From that point on, he continued to use the necklace to get out of bed one time every evening, but his parents could live with that.

Sometimes, bedtime problems are complicated by fears. Remember the story of Philip (pages 49–50)? His fears were actually garden-variety. Getting him over the hump was not difficult. With some kids, however, bedtime fears are part and parcel of a larger "fear complex." That was the case with Nevada.

Nevada was four years old. Her parents were desperate to get her to stay in bed through the night. When they tucked her in, she would begin crying for them to stay in the room with her. If they tried to leave the room, she would become hysterical. One of them usually ended up staying with her until she fell asleep.

But the problem didn't end there. During the day, Nevada was afraid to be in a room by herself, even her own room. She followed her mother around the house, from one room to another, even into the bathroom. And if Nevada wanted to go to the bathroom, she insisted that her mother accompany her. The problem had come on suddenly, three months before the parents sought my advice, and they could not identify anything unusual that had taken place in the family's life before the problem started.

It was obvious to me that being scared of going to sleep by herself and following her mother around the house during the day were one problem, not two. Because the bedtime problem was complicated by fear of separation, traditional punishment was not the solution. In fact, it might well have backfired or made matters worse.

Concerning fears, parents need to understand three things:

1. The more parents talk to a child about her fears, the worse they will get. Even asking a child to explain why she is fearful may backfire. Talk, even compassionate talk, does nothing but feed the Fear Beasties.

2. It is impossible—and I mean impossible—to talk a child out of fears. Even saying things like "There's no such thing as monsters" is an exercise in futility. No child has ever responded to such reassurances with, "Really? No monsters? Gee whiz, Mom and Dad, thanks! I'm not afraid anymore!" So save your breath.

3. Trying to figure out why the child is afraid—trying to "psycho-analyze" the problem, in other words—will only result in half-baked

pseudopsychological theories that will paralyze your ability to deal effectively with the problem.

So I told Nevada's parents to stop trying to understand her fears, stop asking her questions about them, and stop trying to talk her out of them.

"If Nevada wants to talk about them, fine," I said, "but just listen. Don't say anything other than, 'Well, sweetie, sometimes these things just happen to children, and just as fast as they happen, they go away.'"

My next recommendation surprised them. I told them to put up no resistance when Nevada followed them around the house or wanted one of them to lie down with her or go to the bathroom with her. At this point, I brought my old buddy the Doctor in on the case.

I told Nevada's parents: "Tell Nevada you spoke to the Doctor about the problem and that he said she can make three such requests a day. (Note: The quota is arbitrary. If you wish, you can give a child five such "passes" a day to begin with and reduce them as she begins to improve.) Each time she asks you to accompany her into a room, follows you from one room to another so as not to let you out of her sight, or asks you to lie down with her or go to the bathroom with her, she uses a pass. On those occasions, say to her, for example, 'If I go to the bathroom with you, you'll use one of your passes and only have two left. Do you want to use a pass?' She may have second thoughts. (Note: the child's passes can be in the form of tickets. Each time the child uses a pass, she gives her parent a ticket.)

"At first, however, the likelihood is she will use up her free passes fairly quickly. The fourth time she makes one of these requests of you, or follows you around, she loses all of her privileges for the rest of the day—that would include television and all other electronics—and she has to go to bed right after supper. If she exceeds her free passes after supper, then she has to go to bed immediately. Remember, the Doctor said so."

I emphasized the importance of not presenting this as punishment. The Doctor had simply said that her fears meant she wasn't getting enough sleep (the Doctor's usual gambit), and the more fearful she is, the more sleep she needs to help her get over her fears.

"Should one of us still lie down with her?" Nevada's mom asked.

"Yes," I said, "but if she asks you to lie down with her, that means she uses the next day's first free pass and starts the day with two instead of three. In that case, you need to remind her when she gets up the next day that she only has two free passes left."

Less than a week later, the parents called with a progress report. Nevada was usually using one pass at bedtime, one during the day, and then one after supper. In other words, within one week she had gone from exhibiting fears all day long to asking for help with her anxieties only three times in a twenty-four-hour period. Her parents told me she seemed to be aware of how many passes she had left and was using them very selectively, which simply meant that Nevada was achieving mastery of her fears. The concept of "passes" had given her the means to get control over something that had, until that point, controlled her.

With the Doctor's support, Nevada continued to make progress. Within a month, her Fear Beasties had given up and left, never to be heard from again. The success of this sort of approach (and I've seen it succeed many, many times) proves that while a child may be more intelligent than her parents, she is not smarter.

Does anyone have any questions?

Q & A

Q: Our three-year-old is waking up anywhere from two to five times a night (on a bad night, about every two hours). She comes to our room crying. We simply tell her it's still nighttime and walk her back to her bed. She immediately goes back to bed and back to sleep. Sometimes all we have to do is tell her to go back to bed and she will put herself back to sleep. How can we get this to stop?

A: It is not unusual for a child's sleep patterns to change dramatically during late toddlerhood. The child may begin taking fewer naps, taking longer to fall asleep or—as in this case—waking up periodically during the night. When a toddler wakes up in the night crying, just comfort. Do not ask questions. Reassure the child that all is well, that you're taking care of business. Get the child back to sleep as soon as possible, in her own bed. When parents bring the child into bed with them or get in the child's bed, the likelihood of night-waking becoming a difficult-to-undo habit is greatly increased.

The solution: At her bedtime, stretch a ribbon across the doorway to your daughter's room. Locate it such that she'll run into it (chest height) if she walks out of her room in the middle of the night. Tell her that when she feels the ribbon, she's to go back to bed. Rehearse the procedure at least once. Now, this is not going to work magic. Getting it to work is going to take calm, authoritative persistence on your part. When she wakes up and comes into your room, simply take her back to her room, point out the ribbon, and remind her that the ribbon means "get back in bed and go back to sleep." In a week or so, this should be history.

Q: **My sons are four and two. After lunch, I put the youngest to bed for a nap, wait until he's asleep, and then put the oldest down for one as well. The problem is that when I take the oldest upstairs, he raises such a ruckus that he often wakes his younger brother and I have to start over from square one. If I punish him by, say, taking away his favorite blanket, he begins to throw a full-blown fit. I am fine with letting him work through the fit on his own, but that wakes his brother, and around and around we go. I usually end up promising that we'll do something special after his nap, and that generally calms him down. Have**

you any ideas on what I could do to get off this merry-go-round?

A: You will probably have to sacrifice your younger child's nap for up to a week before this merry-go-round stops turning, but I see no other way to accomplish what you want to accomplish. Sit Mr. Disruptive down before his next nap, after his younger brother has gone to sleep, and say something along these lines: "It's time for your nap. I've decided that you can throw a fit if you like. I'm not going to try and stop you, so you have my permission to throw the wildest, loudest fit you've ever thrown. Scream and yell like someone is hurting you if you'd like, but if you wake your younger brother, you will have to stay in your room for the rest of the day and go to bed right after dinner. Do you have any questions? No? Then let's go!"

Without further ado, take him upstairs, put him down, give him a kiss, tell him you love him, and walk out of his room without a look back. If he begins to scream, and he probably will, keep walking. If his younger brother wakes up, tend to him in whatever way seems appropriate, but do not pay the least bit of attention to the dramatics coming from the other room. When Mr. Disruptive's naptime is over, and whether he has gone to sleep or not, simply tell him that he woke his brother and remind him of his punishment. That will undoubtedly begin another fit, in which case you should keep repeating this mantra: "This too will pass, this too will pass, this too will pass . . ." In any case, you absolutely must stop negotiating with him when he starts his meltdown, by which I mean you must stop threatening, promising, persuading, and so on.

The three keys to the success of this venture are that you (1) inform him in advance of the new rule, (2) make no attempt to stop his fit once it starts, and (3) follow through nonchalantly. As I said, this may require that you sacrifice the younger one's nap for a few days, but the price will be well worth paying in the long run. (This same "formula" works quite well across a broad range of discipline problems, by the way.)

Q: **What do you think of parents and children sleeping together?**

A: I am an outspoken opponent of what's called "co-sleeping" or the "family bed." While this arrangement may seem warm and fuzzy, it often devolves into chaos. Despite the claims of "family bed" advocates, not one study done by an objective researcher has demonstrated benefit in either the short or long term to the children so bedded. The American Academy of Pediatrics recommends against the practice, noting that infants are sometimes smothered by parents who inadvertently roll over on them in the night or as a result of getting tangled in the large sheets and blankets.

It's almost always the mother who has bought into the propaganda that this promotes parent-child bonding. And if other moms in her social group are bedding with their kids, she feels the additional pressure of not wanting to be the most "unbonded" mom in the neighborhood. But there is no two ways about it: a child who sleeps with his parents develops a dependency upon sleeping with his parents, one that comes back to haunt all concerned when the parents decide the child's presence in the bed has become inconvenient. Meanwhile, this child has been deprived of the inestimable benefit of learning that he was not a member of the wedding, that the marriage is not a threesome.

Q: **My problem involves three-year-old twin boys who have learned to climb out of their cribs, thus turning bedtime into a two-hour play-fest. They have a gate in their doorway so they can't roam the house, but they are up playing until ten o'clock. Do you have any suggestions on how to keep them in their beds?**

A: You should let your boys be boys at bedtime. As John Eldredge has pointed out in his book of the same name, males are "wild at heart" and need appropriate outlets for their wildness. Why is it important to you that these fun-loving boys, who obviously have a wonderful relationship, stay in their beds (or, in the meantime, their cribs)? I believe I am correct in assuming that during their play-fest, they don't stand at the gate and scream for you. And when they have had their fill of play-festing, they fall asleep on their own, right? And they sleep through the night, yes? And they don't seem any the worse for it the next day, yes? The operative principle here is "If it ain't broke, don't try to fix it." Can you say "earplugs"?

Q: What do you think of letting older kids "sleep in" on weekends? Our son, age twelve, will sleep until lunch if we let him. My husband thinks this is ridiculous, that he needs to be kept on a schedule. I think he needs to catch up on his sleep. Have any studies been done on this?

A: I'm not aware of any studies that have been done on the relative effect of letting preteens and teenagers sleep as long as they want on non-school days as opposed to making them get up early, but recent studies have found that many, if not most, preteens and teens are not getting nearly enough sleep. Sleep deprivation depresses school performance, is a cause of stress, and lowers performance levels on mechanical tasks, such as driving a car. The only reason this age child would need to "catch up" on his sleep (a myth, as lost sleep is lost, forever) is if he isn't getting enough during the week. That's called sleep deprivation, in which case I strongly encourage you to put limits on how late he can stay up on school nights. (Helpful hint: remove the television and computer from his room until he's managing his time better.)

FOOD FIGHTS

A 2009 television commercial shows a mom using the video feature on her phone to learn how to fix paella. She then text-messages her teenage son to tell him that's what they're having for dinner. He sends back a video message saying, "I don't know what 'pah-ella' is, but I'm *not* eating it!" With a smile and a chuckle, the mother uses her phone to order a pizza for her spoiled, rude, self-centered, ungrateful son.

Many of today's parents seem confused over the meaning of the term "family meal." Allow me to explain. The term *meal* refers to prepared food. A "family" is a group of adults and children who share one or more of the following: genes, living space, possessions, goals, and values. The operative word is *share*.

A *family* meal, therefore, is a shared occasion. When a family sits down to eat, and one member of the family is served a meal that differs from what the other members of the family are consuming (without medical justification, such as a verified allergy), the family is no longer sharing; therefore, that occasion no longer qualifies as a *family* meal. One member of the family is being treated as if he or she is a special case, deserving of special considerations. That family member is being treated, in effect, as if he is not a member of the family. The previous three sentences are descriptive of what is happening in all too many American households these days. And then parents wonder why their children are picky eaters. Now hang on tight, because the next paragraph may seem to completely contradict what I just said, but it does not, and I will explain why not in a moment.

Adding to the problem of picky eaters is the nouveau practice of seating infants and toddlers at the "big table" during family meals. This gives the young child a platform from which to garner a disproportionate amount of attention and greatly increases the likelihood of food fights. The attention referred to consists of repeated attempts on the part of the young child's parents to get said young child to eat certain foods, as in the following all-too-typical examples:

- "Alfie, why don't you just try eating some turnipseed puree? It's good for you! It will help you become a smart, strong boy! C'mon, take just one bite, okay?"

- "If you eat just one bite of those green, shiny things, you can have a bowl of special ice cream after supper! Whataya say? They have vitamins in them, and children who don't eat vitamins don't grow. They stay small forever. You want to grow, don't you?"

- "Here [reaching over and moving food around on child's plate]. Now, just eat the food I've put on this side of the plate, okay? That's all you have to eat. It's not much. It's not even enough to keep a mouse alive. Honey? You really have to eat something. You'll just dry up and blow away in the wind if you don't eat. Please eat something for Mommy, okay? Here [moving more food around]. Just eat that one bite of roast beef. Okay? Honey, I don't know what I'm going to do with you. You're at the fifth percentile, and you need to eat something. What can I fix you that you'll eat? Just tell Mommy and I'll fix it. Blueberry pancakes? No? How about a peanut-butter-and-jelly sandwich?"

In each of these all-too-typical scenarios, the child in question sits at the center of attention at the ersatz "family" meal, orchestrating the "I don't like that" drama. Eventually, the parents concede defeat and begin fixing the child special meals. The "family" has roast beef, mashed potatoes, gravy, and a salad for supper. Prince Robbie the Ungrateful has a corn dog and French fries. His vegetable is ketchup—a special ketchup that comes in a Barney bottle. He washes it all down with a highly caffeinated, highly sugar-sweetened soda that helps keep him up until midnight. Did I tell you he won't go to bed cooperatively either?

All of this silliness is preventable. The way to keep food fights with a child from ever getting started is to follow these simple rules:

- As soon as the child graduates from baby food, serve him what everyone else in the family is being served.

- As long as the child is in a high chair, feed him separately, before everyone else sits down to eat. By the age of twelve months, you should give him only a sippy to drink from—no more bottles (and end the sippy by eighteen months). When he's done, put him down and send him off to play.

- As soon as your child learns to eat without getting food all over him and his surroundings, sit him in his own little chair at his own little table set over in the corner of the kitchen. Serve him first, and let him finish what he wants to eat before you serve the big people. Don't hover over him while he eats (or doesn't). Don't encourage him to eat, even. Simply tell him that when he's had enough, he should go find something to do while everyone else has their meal. This does not send the message to the child that he isn't wanted or some other such psychobabblistic drivel. Children love their own little table and chair. Take it from me. I sat at a little table, in my little chair, until I was four or five and ready to learn good manners. I do not need therapy for this. To this day, I eat anything and everything that's put on my plate. I am not a Special Case.

- During the day, let your toddler graze. Leave a platter of finger food and a cup of water out, all day long, at his level. To those folks who think infants should get used to eating with the rest of the family, I say there's a time for everything, and this is not the time. If a child does not eat with the family, until age four or five, he will civilize quickly when he does. Besides, that's four or five years of invaluable mealtime peace.

- If you insist upon having your little one at the Big Table so that he doesn't feel unloved and develop a lifelong psychiatric disorder, fine. (Don't say I didn't warn you.) Just do yourself and him a huge favor and serve him the same food everyone else is eating. If he says he doesn't like it and isn't going to eat it, just say, "Fine, you may be excused." Don't encourage him or bribe him to eat or otherwise make an issue of what he doesn't want to eat. If he leaves food on his plate, just cover it and put it aside. If he asks for food later in the evening, saying he's hungry, tell him you saved his supper. Heat it up in the microwave and serve it to him again, making it clear that he gets nothing else until he's finished what he was originally served.

- If your child asks why he has to eat things he doesn't like, say, "Because I am training you to be a good guest in someone else's home. It is rude to refuse to eat what someone else cooked unless you have a true allergy to the food. You have no food allergies that I know of, so you need to learn to eat what you are served." Period. Short 'n' sweet.

A number of years ago, I was consulted by the parents of a ten-year-old girl who felt that she should be catered to at mealtimes. Whenever the family sat down to a meal, she began complaining. Her mother told me that trying to persuade her to take even one bite of something she had decided was offensive was "worse than pulling teeth." On several occasions, after the parents insisted that she eat something she didn't want to eat, she ran to the bathroom and threw up. They had tried making her sit at the table until she ate everything on her plate, but she had successfully waited them out. Obviously, food had become a huge issue in this little girl's life. Mom admitted that she had often just given in and fixed her daughter a special meal to ensure that she was getting proper nutrition.

First, I redefined the situation. "This has nothing to do with nutrition," I said. "She's obviously not wasting away. She eats what she's served at breakfast and lunch. She only has a problem at suppertime. Why? Because she's learned that if she creates uproar over food, she can be the center of attention at family meals. This is about her manners and her proper place in the family."

I went on: "It is rude to complain about food that someone else has prepared. It is equally rude to refuse to eat it because of some neurotic prejudice. Do you want your daughter going to someone else's home and complaining about food her hosts prepare for her? Then don't allow her to complain about the food *you* prepare.

"With regard to her place in the family, must I remind you that she is a child? By allowing her to disrupt family meals with her complaints, by pleading with her to eat, by fixing her special food, you are aiding and abetting her grasp for prominence within the family. As long as she can control the family by whining and complaining at the dinner table, she will."

After my (calm but purposeful) rant, I told the parents to serve her a plate with ridiculously small portions of the same foods everyone else in the family would be eating—one forkful of each item. They were then to inform her of the first of two new rules: she had to eat *everything* in order to get seconds of *anything*. Mind you, "everything" was three forkfuls of foulness.

Her parents told her she didn't have to eat anything she didn't want to eat. If she left food on her plate, however, her mother wrapped it and set it aside. If the child later complained of being hungry, Mom just unwrapped her unfinished dinner and gave it back to her, saying, "When you finish this, you can have anything you want."

Here's where the second of the two new rules kicked in: she did not have to eat, but she was not to complain about anything on her plate. If she complained, after-supper privileges were taken away and her bedtime was moved up one hour.

I emphasized the importance of not making remarks about what she ate or didn't eat and not trying to persuade her to eat. I told her parents to pay no more attention to her than they would if she was not a picky eater. If she ate everything, she was allowed to have a second portion of any food or foods that were originally on her plate, and the second portions could be as large as she wanted.

Finally, I said, "If she acts like she's going to throw up after eating something, simply tell her to go to the bathroom. When she returns, inform her that throwing up or acting like she has to is tantamount to a nonverbal complaint and earns the same punishment—early bedtime."

This little girl tested the new rules with all of the energy her nutritionally deprived body could muster. She complained (and was sent to bed early), refused to eat (and went hungry), and threw up (and was sent to bed early). Two weeks of drama went by, and then she began eating. At that point, I told the parents not to praise her or pay any more attention to the fact that she was eating than they paid to what each other was eating. Within a month, the problem was solved. And the girl lived on to invent more drama, I'm sure.

STEALING AND LYING (AND OTHER DECEITS)

There are lots of pseudopsychological myths floating around concerning children, one of which is the myth of the manipulative child. This bit of whimsy proposes that children do perplexing, problematic things in order to get other people to give them their way, control other people, control their families, draw attention to themselves, and the like.

When a psychologist tells parents that their child is "being manipulative," he sounds more brilliant than if he said, "I have no idea why your child is doing what he's doing. There's no way I can explain his behavior with any degree of confidence." But in most cases, that would be the truth. Furthermore, "manipulative" means the problem lies *inside* the child, buried somewhere deep in the child's psyche, which means the child needs therapy! So, by using the word *manipulative*, the psychologist *manipulates* the child's parents into paying him a lot of money for therapy sessions that may or may not result in any progress and may in fact make the problem worse.

The ability to manipulate people requires fairly sophisticated mental aptitude. It requires that the child in question possess the ability to analyze the effect his behavior is having on other people. It requires the ability to plan ahead in conspiratorial fashion, as in, "I'm going to begin complaining of a headache now because I know from past experience that when I complain of physical problems, my mother gives me sympathy, pampers me, and is more likely to do what I want her to do." The best research into cognitive development finds that those abilities don't emerge until some-time around age twelve, give or take a year. In other words, children don't possess the brainpower to be truly, deviously manipulative until they are on the cusp of adolescence.

Before age twelve, it may at times *seem* like a child is manipulating his parents: when he does A, they reliably respond by doing B. But the key to manipulation is *intention*, and eight-year-olds, for example, lack that degree of wherewithal. So if intention isn't there, then the fact that A results in B is nothing but a bad family habit. It's no more the child's *doing* than the fact that shortly after he wakes up in the morning, his parents serve him breakfast. Getting up in the morning isn't the child's way of *manipulating* his parents into serving breakfast. It's just the way things are in that family. It's a family habit; in this example, a functional one.

Curiosity Thrilled the Kat

All of this brings to mind a little girl whose parents sought my help a number of years ago. Katharine—"Kat" to her family and friends—was six at the time. The problem was that she took things from her parents. To be more precise, she *stole*. She took without permission, hid the items she took, and when confronted, denied having taken them. That's a fair definition of stealing, wouldn't you agree? Most of the things Kat stole belonged to her mother—makeup, jewelry, fashion accessories. Occasionally, however, Kat pilfered from her father—chewing gum, a pocketknife, sunglasses, and anything else he might leave lying around.

Whenever something mysteriously disappeared, Kat's parents would confront her. They would ask if she took it, and she would say she didn't. At this point, the game of "Scotland Yard" would begin. Her parents would give Kat the third degree, but she would refuse to confess. Then they would search Kat's room and any other rooms she had recently spent time in. Eventually, they would find the missing item. Sometimes it took mere minutes; sometimes it took days. After her parents found the loot, Kat would confess. Her explanation was always the same: "I just wanted to look at it."

"But why didn't you just ask if you could look at it?" her parents would ask.

And Kat, looking down at the floor, would answer, "I don't know."

"Why did you hide it?" her parents would ask.

And Kat, still looking at the floor, would answer, "I don't know." And then she would begin to cry, sobbing that she was sorry and wouldn't do it again. But she would, within several days.

Her parents were at wit's end. They didn't know what to think or even how to feel about Kat's stealing. Sometimes, they would become angry at her. After being angry, they'd end up feeling guilty because it began to seem as if Kat *couldn't help* what she was doing. It seemed as if some force inside of her was making her steal things. After all, she always seemed contrite when she was caught.

They went to see a psychologist. After two sessions spent talking mostly with Kat, the psychologist told the parents that Kat was stealing in order to manipulate them. She was manipulating them, he said, to gain control of the family, be the center of attention. Furthermore, the objects she stole represented the parents' love, which she was unsure of.

The *American Heritage Dictionary of the English Language*, Third Edition, defines *manipulate* thus: "to influence or manage shrewdly or deviously."

This psychologist was proposing that Kat, age six, shrewdly conspired to control her parents. Hogfeathers! Kat wasn't plotting to take over her family. She felt just as confused about the problem as her parents. When she said she didn't know why she took things from her parents, she was telling the truth.

I didn't know why either. When Kat's parents asked me that question, I said, "I have no idea why Kat is stealing things from you. There's no way I can answer that question with any degree of confidence."

In my estimation, the stealing-and-sleuthing cycle was just a bad habit the family had gotten into somewhat by accident. Most kids experiment with stealing at some time or another, and the first people they steal from are usually their parents. For unknown reasons, some kids stop after being caught and punished, but some kids keep doing it. The attempt to explain it is fruitless. The issue, therefore, is not *why* it's happening. The issue is how to stop it from happening, how to break the family's bad habit.

This is one of those behavior problems that punishment alone won't solve. It's usually appropriate to punish a child for stealing, mind you, but a more creative approach is called for.

I told Kat's parents that to break the stealing-and-sleuthing cycle, they had to stop playing Scotland Yard. I had them put a box in Kat's room labeled MOM'S AND DAD'S THINGS. Next, they stopped using the word "stealing" and began instead to use the word "curiosity." They told Kat that she had their permission to be curious about their things.

They said, "Whenever you're curious about something of ours, and you want to hold it and look at it, just put it in this box when you're done." And that was that. No more hand-wringing, no more sleuthing, no more third degree. Just put it in the box.

From then on, if something turned up missing, they went into Kat's room and looked in the box. Usually, it was there. If not, instead of asking questions (the first move in "Scotland Yard"), they made a statement such as, "Kat, I need my earrings back, please." Lo and behold, Kat would give them back!

Within a few weeks, Kat stopped taking things from her parents. If she wanted to look at something, she would ask. And they would give it to her, and she would look at it, and then she would give it back. And that was that.

That's my usual modus operandi when it comes to kids who steal. Nine out of ten times, the box in the back hall is all it takes. Sometimes, however, a little more . . . shall we say, *force* is necessary.

A Criminal-in-the-Making

One such example involved Rachel, a nine-year-old girl who'd been adopted at age three from Romania. Although she'd fared well in all respects, Rachel was a thief. Like Kat, she stole from her parents. But she also stole from her teachers, other people's houses, and kids at school. Whenever her parents confronted her, she denied having taken the item in question. When it showed up later among her possessions (as it always did), she claimed not to know how it got there. Complicating matters, a therapist had told the parents that Rachel's stealing was symptomatic of "unresolved attachment issues." In other words, Rachel hadn't bonded to her adoptive parents, and every incident of stealing was more evidence of that.

This is pure, refined psychobabble. The therapist could not have proven that Rachel had attachment issues. It was just a convenient thing for him to say. Plus, it made him sound like he had the ability to peer into Rachel's psyche and see things hidden from people who didn't have impressive degrees. In the long run, the therapist's psychobabble only served to make Rachel's parents feel like complete failures.

Ultimately, they came to me for help. Because Rachel was stealing from other people, I doubted that the box in the back hall, by itself, was going to work. But I gave it a try anyway. In this case, it was just labeled THINGS RACHEL FOUND. As I suspected might happen, things continued to go missing yet nothing showed up in the box.

The good news was that despite her bad habit (and everyone seemed to be aware of it), Rachel was well liked and very social. She was always getting invitations to come to other kids' houses for parties, sleepovers, play dates, and so on. She was a nine-year-old socialite.

I say Rachel's social nature was good news because it gave us the force we needed. It was apparent that nothing short of activating the Agony and Godfather Principles was going to work with Rachel. Here's what her "therapy" looked like:

1. Instead of a Target Misbehavior List, I had her parents put a Missing Things List on the refrigerator. When they discovered that something was missing, and they were reasonably sure they'd not misplaced it, they were to simply add it to the list. They weren't to even ask Rachel if she had it. She could read.

2. When they realized something was missing, I told them to act nonchalant. They weren't even to ask her if she had the item in question. Just put it on the list.

3. They were to tell Rachel's teacher to report missing items. Furthermore, when she went over to someone else's house, they were to call and ask the parents to inform them of any missing items. Those went on the list as well.

4. Then, they made a rule: as long as there was even one item on the list, Rachel would not be allowed to participate in any after-school activities, go to friends' houses, or have friends over, and they would not buy her anything except what was absolutely essential.

5. Her parents maintained the RETURNS box in the back hall and told Rachel that when the item (or items) on the list showed up in the box, her privileges would be restored. This allowed her to atone without a big deal being made of it.

If, while Rachel's life was "suspended," she protested her innocence, her parents were to simply say, "We're not going to talk about it. The rule is the rule." Likewise, when a missing something showed up in the box, they just crossed it off the list without fanfare. This is not, mind you, a quick fix. Nonetheless, my experience has been that this method slowly but surely causes (or allows) a child's stealing to die a natural death, but the operative word is *slowly*. Rachel tried everything she could to beat the system, but because her parents maintained their complete cool, she eventually gave up and discovered that honesty is the best of all policies.

Ask Them No Questions and They'll Tell You No Lies

Why do children lie? The answer: because they are human. God's children have been lying from the very beginning. So let's get something straight: if your child is a habitual liar, it's not because he feels unloved or because you're not giving him enough attention or because his self-esteem is low (because he feels unloved and you're not giving him enough attention). No, those are examples of psychobabble. But I do know one thing: when a child tells a lie and his parents get all bent out of shape, the child is that much likelier to tell another lie. Why? Because the parents have created a drama in which the child is the central figure. Under the circumstances, the child will hold out as long as he can because the longer he holds out, the longer he occupies the center of attention.

Being the central character in a family soap opera is highly addicting. In many a family, there's a person who can't seem to stop doing stupid, self-destructive things. In almost every case, if you go back into that person's history, the problem began in childhood. It may have started small, but from the very beginning it threw everyone into a tizzy—the start of a family soap opera. A disproportionate amount of attention, concern, and agitation was directed toward the child, who quickly found himself at the center of an emotional cyclone. Who doesn't want to be the star of the show? The problem is that a child who is the star of the Lying Game quickly becomes addicted to lying. This happens the same way a person gets addicted to gambling: every so often, the child "wins" the Lying Game. That's all it takes.

It's vital, therefore, that the Lying Game never get started. When a child tells a lie, everyone needs to keep their cool. In addition, everyone needs to keep what I call "apocalyptic thinking" under control. Lying doesn't mean a child is headed for a life of crime, or politics.

If the Lying Game is already in full swing, the way out is to keep in mind the adage "Ask them no questions, they'll tell you no lies." Invariably, the parents of a lying child are asking questions when they already know the answer. A mother once told me that her nine-year-old daughter had started lying about small things. When I asked for an example, she told me that just the day before, her daughter had lied about chewing gum. It was obvious she had gum in her mouth, but she denied it.

"What exactly happened?" I asked.

"Well," the mother replied, "I noticed she had gum in her mouth so

I asked, 'Do you have gum in your mouth?' and she said she didn't. And that started it. I said 'It looks like you have gum in your mouth' and she insisted she didn't, so I told her to open her mouth and she refused and then began to complain that I never believe her, which is garbage. We went back and forth like this for about three minutes, maybe longer, before she finally admitted it and spit it out."

That's a perfect description of the Lying Game. The mother knew the child had gum in her mouth, but instead of simply saying, "Please spit out your gum," she asked a foolish question. The question invites a lie. If a state trooper pulled you over and asked, "Excuse me, but were you speeding?" would you admit it if you had been? C'mon! Be honest! The closest you'd come to telling the truth would be, "I don't think so." That's why state troopers, when they pull you over, simply say, "I stopped you because you were speeding." If they ask no questions, speeders are far less likely to tell lies.

The mother's foolish question started the Lying Game, which is a variation on the game of cat and mouse. The mouse (the daughter) steals the cheese (the truth). She taunts the mother with it, and the mother starts chasing her around the proverbial house. Even though the mother eventually catches the daughter in the lie and takes the cheese away, the game is very exciting and as addictive as any other form of gambling.

I explained all this to the mother, emphasized the importance of the "ask them no questions" rule, and told her to give me a progress report in two weeks. Two weeks passed and she didn't call. I waited a few days and then called her. She told me she'd completely forgotten.

"Just like you told me," she said, "as soon as I stopped asking foolish questions, my daughter stopped telling foolish lies."

In this child's case, her mother was able to stop the Lying Game before it gained a lot of momentum. More often than not, however, the game is running at full speed when it comes to my attention. The child's lies are legion, and the lies themselves are much more serious than denying there's gum in the mouth.

"His Pants Were On Fire!"

Ruben was one such child. By the time he came to my attention, he was ten. His parents told me he'd been lying since he was six. The first lies were about school. He would say he had a good day when, in reality, he had gotten into trouble. He'd say he had no homework when he had quite a bit. And so on. Ruben quickly became the star of the Lying Game, and his lying got progressively worse. By the time I got involved, he was lying about nearly everything, and his parents told me they'd tried nearly everything. They'd taken away his favorite toys, his favorite privileges, his ability to have or go to sleepovers. They had him sit in a chair until he decided to tell the truth (he would sit for hours). They had him write sentences like "I won't tell any more lies to my parents." They had even rewarded him for not lying. Ruben just kept right on lying. He was what's called a "hard case."

The first thing I got the parents to do was simply calm down. To great degree, their agitation reflected their unspoken feeling that Ruben was lying because they were bad parents of some sort. We were able to talk that through fairly easily, and they were able to relax. The second thing they had to get rid of was the feeling that Ruben was a hopeless case. I explained that Ruben was addicted to lying in the same way that some adults are addicted to gambling. As such, he needed to be rescued. That changed their whole point of view. The next thing I got them to do was stop asking questions when they already knew the answer or were 90 percent sure of it. Sure enough, within a couple of weeks, Ruben's lying was half of what it had been. Once the parents had calmed down, quit regarding Ruben as a felon, and stopped asking foolish questions, the actual rescue effort could start.

I told them that whenever they were 90 percent sure Ruben had told a lie, they were to begin a scripted exchange by simply asking, "Why are you doing that?" Here's how a typical exchange would go:

"Hey, Ruben. Whatcha been up to?"

"I was over at Kenny's house."

(At this point red flags go off for Ruben's mom, who was just at Kenny's house herself, dropping something off with Kenny's mom.)

"Ruben, why are you doing that?"

Ruben would look startled and say, "Doing what?"

"I'm not going to play the game, Ruben. I love you too much."

Ruben would say, "What game?" or "I'm not playing any game!"

Mom would then say, "This conversation is officially over," and walk away.

In that way, Ruben's parents starved Ruben's lies of drama. No cat and mouse, no hand wringing, no agitation, no attempts to get to the bottom of things, no punishment. They simply let Ruben know that they knew he was lying and let it go.

At first, Ruben acted indignant. "You always think I'm lying!" he would shout, to which his parents would say, "The conversation is officially over." I told them that they must not ever become involved in any arguments with Ruben over whether he had or had not been lying.

"But what if we later find out he was telling the truth?" they asked.

"Then just go to him and tell him you've discovered he was telling the truth, and tell him you appreciate that, and let that be it."

"Should we tell him we're sorry?"

"No, because you shouldn't be sorry," I said. "Ruben has created this problem, not you. You should simply acknowledge your mistake and let that be it. No drama, remember? Besides, you're going to find that you're hardly ever wrong."

I want to point out, once again, that while there's a time and place for punishment, punishment is but one option when it comes to misbehavior. My experience has convinced me that lying and stealing don't respond to punishment. It's as if the deceptive child regards punishment as a challenge. The bigger the punishment, the more determined the child becomes to stick to his story and refuse to confess.

Within a couple of weeks, Ruben's lying, already cut by half, was cut by half again. The excitement had gone out of the game. As Ruben began telling the truth more often than lying, he began to discover that life without the false excitement of the Lying Game was a whole lot more satisfying. He began to realize, intuitively, how much time and energy he'd been wasting on lying, and he began to put his energies into more productive pursuits. Within a few months, Ruben's lying was pretty much history, and he was a much, much happier camper.

Is it always that simple? No, but I consistently find that when the habitual liar's parents are able to completely stop their participation in the drama of the Lying Game, the game slowly grinds to a halt.

Q & A

Q: My five-year-old son has a friend, also five, who has recently started lying, or telling stories, about relatively insignificant things. For example, today he informed me, in front of my son, that he got his ears pierced. Of course he didn't, but I played along. When I *have* confronted him, he has insisted he is telling me the truth. He loves to pull his friends and parents into verbal arguments, and I believe that is what he wants to do with me. How should I handle this?

A: First, let me affirm that this child's "stories" do indeed qualify as lies. You are reluctant to call them by their rightful name because the liar in question is five years old. Your big heart notwithstanding, children are quite capable of lying, and what begins as telling tall tales can easily evolve into telling big-time, self-destructive untruths.

In situations of this sort, and especially when the prevaricator in question is young, adults have a tendency to "play along," to not confront the issue. When it's obvious that the child is developing a bad habit, this is most definitely the wrong thing to do. With a three-year-old who can't quite tell the difference between reality and the products of his or her fertile imagination, playing along is fine and fun. But playing along with a five-year-old is potentially damaging to the child's social health, and the more people wear kid gloves with this child concerning this issue, the worse it is likely to get.

So the next time he tells you a tall tale, just look at him and say, without rancor, but very straightforwardly, "No, you didn't" or, "Do you really think I believe that?" Then, regardless of what he says, do not engage in further discussion (argument). Just turn around and walk away. That may seem cold, but it is truly the kindest thing you can possibly do.

Q: **We grounded our twelve-year-old daughter because she watched an R-rated movie with a girlfriend while we were out for the evening. Her defense is that she told us the name of the movie before we left and we said it was okay. That's true, but she knows that R movies are off-limits in our house and left out that vital piece of information on purpose. Now she won't talk to us. I know how important it is to keep open communication, so I'm now thinking I shouldn't fight this battle. Have we done the right thing, or should we drop it?**

A: I think your daughter is very clever. She knew exactly what she was doing when she asked if she and her girlfriend could watch the movie. In legalese, withholding vital evidence is equivalent to lying. Caught, she now plays the victim. Clever again! You did the right thing. Stand your ground, stick to your guns, hang tough, and so on.

As for keeping open communication with a preteen, that's a two-way street and a shared responsibility. Your daughter violated the bond of trust that is prerequisite to good parent-child communication. It is not your responsibility to fix something that you did not break. Besides, the silent treatment is pure drama, part of your daughter's victim act, not indication that there is a communication problem between you. Furthermore, sooner or later, she's going to have to ask you for something, at which point she will talk. In the meantime, welcome the vacation.

SIBLING WARFARE

Let's get something straight right off the bat. There's a difference between sibling conflict and sibling rivalry. Sibling conflict is inevitable. The only two ways of preventing it are to (1) have only one child, and (2) space your children eighteen years apart.

The sibling relationship is unlike most other relationships because siblings do not choose each other. They're simply thrown together. Sometimes the chemistry works and sometimes it doesn't. Some siblings have a lot of conflict, and some have little, but all siblings have some degree of conflict. It's as inevitable as marital conflict. Just as two married people have things they have to work out, so do siblings. But I would hope that adults are able to work things out in a more civil fashion than children.

Sibling conflict becomes sibling *rivalry* when you, the well-intentioned parent, get involved in an attempt to end the conflict. Inevitably, your intervention causes you to appear to side with the sibling who was "done wrong" by the other sibling. In other words, when you get involved in sibling conflict, the *victim* wins, and three things happen:

1. Your children learn that playing the role of victim has benefits. Obviously, that's not a good thing. It can, in fact, become a lifelong burden. If you know someone who constantly plays the role of victim, there's a fair chance that habit got its start when he or she was a child, within the context of a sibling conflict situation.

2. The designated victim, because he "wins," and because he experiences the pleasure of seeing you reprimand his sibling, begins to try to entice the "bad" sibling into conflict.

3. The designated villain feels wronged and begins to seek ways of retaliating against the designated victim without being caught

doing so. Or he seeks to create conflict situations in which he looks like the victim.

A vicious cycle quickly forms within which the children begin competing for the coveted Victim Award.

The first thing you need to come to grips with concerning sibling conflict is that it's virtually inevitable. Furthermore, siblings are more likely to have conflict than spouses, and considerably more than friends, given that friends don't usually live together. The long and short of all this is you can't mandate that siblings have affection for one another. The good news is most siblings put their childhood differences aside as adults and become as close as their personalities will allow.

Whereas parents can't stop siblings from having conflict, they can take steps to effectively contain the level of conflict. Here are the steps involved in accomplishing this:

1. Create a "Do Not Disturb the Family Peace" rule: The children can have conflict, but they must (a) keep it down, (b) not engage in physical aggression of any kind toward one another, and (c) not tattle on one another, even in instances of physical aggression.
2. Put the rule on an index card and magnetize it to the refrigerator door. It should look something like this:

Do Not Disturb the Family Peace

- Keep your conflict to yourselves. Do not disturb anyone else with it.

- Do not complain to Mom or Dad about one another.

- Make no attempt to physically hurt one another.

---

3. Use the "Tickets" or "Strikes" system. Take a ticket or call a strike every time the rule is broken. If you're using Tickets, the kids begin every day with three, no matter how old they are, no matter how serious the problem. If, however, more than two children are actors in the sibling conflict drama, add a ticket for each additional child. Correspondingly, if you're using "Strikes," then you go to four strikes per day for three children, and so on.

4. On any given day, the first time the rule is broken you simply identify the infraction and either take a ticket or call a strike. "You're disturbing the family (or me, or us) with your conflict, so I'm taking a ticket (or calling a strike)." If one of the kids begins complaining about the other, you say, "That's tattling, and I'm taking another ticket (or calling another strike)."

    Read the following carefully; then read it again: If you have more than two children who are involved in the sibling conflict drama (even though only two are involved at any one time), you still have only one set of tickets (or one allowance of strikes.)

    When one child tattles (or screams, or throws something at a sibling), all of the children on the program lose a ticket or incur a strike. You are holding all of the children involved equally responsible for the problem. However, do not include a child younger than three and a half in the program. If you have such a child, you're going to have to deal with him separately, outside of the program. Nonetheless, it's vital that you not give him the impression, ever, that he is his older sibling's victim.

5. When the rule is broken, it's vitally important that you make no attempt to find out what happened or why the kids are arguing. Nor should you make any effort to mediate the conflict. Just issue the penalty and walk away. You can, if you choose (and you are free to choose inconsistently, on a situation-by-situation basis), have the specific offenders sit in separate Chairs of Horrifying Humiliation for fifteen minutes. Give yourself a break if you need one.

6. When the last ticket of the day is taken (or the last strike is called), the children go to their respective rooms for the remainder of the day, and they all go to bed early. As usual, if you're going to be confining them to their rooms, it's helpful to reduce the "entertainment value" of the rooms beforehand. If they share a room, then one child goes to the room and the other child is confined in some other area of the home with a couple of books and perhaps one toy. The next time the penalty is incurred, you switch their places. The child who was confined to the shared bedroom is now confined elsewhere, and vice versa.

Now, let's say you have three kids on the program, and only two of them are involved in any given incident. Nonetheless, all three incur the penalty. All three lose a ticket for the incident or all three incur a strike. Conceivably (this won't happen often), a child who is gone from the home most of the day might come home to discover that he is confined to his room for the remainder of the day because the children who were at home are so confined.

"But that's not fair, John," some reader is saying.

Oh, but it is. The child in that example has been helping to stir the pot of sibling conflict for however long—years, perhaps. The fact that he is gone from the home for the day makes him no less responsible for the problem. This is not a new approach to problems of this sort. In an earlier era, a teacher might keep an entire class in from recess when only one child in the class misbehaved. In so doing, she knew that the class would discipline the offending child for her. Their peer pressure was much more effective a deterrent than anything she might have done. In this case, by putting all of the actors in the sibling conflict drama into the same boat, by holding them *equally* responsible for *every* incident whether they are directly involved in any *one* incident or not, you cause them to begin policing one another. In order to not lose tickets or incur strikes, they have to learn to cooperate in paddling the proverbial boat.

Having said that, I must stress that children who are not involved in the drama are not included in the program. However, if a child who generally stays out of it lets herself get drawn in, deal with her separately. Don't put her on the program simply because she allowed herself to get caught up in one conflict situation that got out of hand.

You might, for whatever reason, not resonate with the Ticket or Strike solution to sibling conflict. If that's the case, then consider using the "Conference Room" technique:

1. Put the "Do Not Disturb the Family Peace" rule on the refrigerator.
2. When the rule is broken, put the offending kids into a "Conference Room" together for fifteen minutes while directing them to use the time to try and solve whatever problem precipitated the incident. I generally recommend that the designated conference room be (a) small so that they can't avoid one another and (b) boring so that they can't distract themselves from the task at hand. A small bathroom ("powder room"), laundry room, mudroom, or guest bedroom will do.
3. So you don't have to be concerned with watching the clock, set a timer outside the door of said Conference Room. When the timer winds down and the alarm goes off, open the door and ask the kids, "Is the problem solved?" They will tell you that it is even if they didn't say a thing to one another, or even look at one another, for the fifteen minutes. That's fine. Let them out and walk away. There's a very, very slim chance that they will tell you it isn't solved. If they do, you simply confine them for another fifteen minutes.

Whether you use Tickets, Strikes, or Conference Room, you are taking yourself out of the equation and putting responsibility for solving the sibling conflict problem squarely on the children's shoulders. The children stop competing for the coveted Victim Award because you're no longer handing it out. The children learn to keep their conflicts to themselves and work them out without your intervention, which is a skill that will carry over nicely to situations later in their lives, including their marriages.

Q & A

Q: **My kids are four and just-turned two. They are having more and more conflict, mostly over toys. Can I use one of the above approaches with them?**

A: Not really. As I said earlier, you can't put a child on Tickets or Strikes until the child is three years, six months old—until, that is, the child is able to predict consequences, able to "think ahead." Until then, you just have to muddle through some things. My book *Making the "Terrible" Twos Terrific* includes a chapter on how to discipline toddlers, given the inherent limitations. In the case of conflict between a toddler and an older sibling, you have several options. You can, when an incident occurs, separate the children and, using a timer, keep them separate for a "cool down" period of fifteen to thirty minutes. You can take the object of their competition—a toy, usually—away from them. Regardless, you are going to have to accept that whatever approach you take is going to have little long-term effect. In the meantime, until you can put Tickets or Strikes or Conference Room into place, it's vitally important that you not set the precedent of identifying one child as the victim and the other as the villain. That does nothing but feed the sibling conflict beast and make it that much more difficult to subdue later.

Q: **We have two boys. One is almost four; the other is twenty months. At first, the older one seemed to accept the younger one and things went well. Within the past few months, however, an often intense rivalry has developed. It's hard to tell who starts something, but the older boy is clearly using his size to his advantage. When they get into a scrap, the older one will knock the younger one down, snatch things away, and has even hit him on several recent occasions. Can you give me some guidelines on how to deal with this?**

A: You're not describing sibling conflict or rivalry; you're describing sibling abuse. Likewise, arguments between husband and wife are one thing; a spouse hitting a spouse is quite another. Your toddler needs your protection, meaning your almost four-year-old needs to be stopped before this pattern becomes any stronger. That's going to require powerful, memorable consequences—ones that embody both the Agony and Godfather Principles. The punishment you use is going to have to be a *lot* more powerful than the payoff the older boy is experiencing when he abuses his brother.

I recommend a zero-tolerance policy here. When the four-year-old gets physical with his brother, don't threaten, remind, or warn. Take him immediately to his room, confine him there for the remainder of the day, and put him to bed right after supper. You should be firm and resolute, but not angry.

Be clear that you will not tolerate him hitting or pushing his brother. The next day, first thing, he must apologize to his brother and give him a hug. If he refuses, keep him in his room until he sees the wisdom of at least *acting* remorseful. Along the way, make sure you keep telling him that the way he can avoid going to his room is to come to you when his brother is upsetting him. Assure him of your help with whatever is making him upset.

The obvious risk of this approach is twofold:

1. The little brother will eventually begin to see that there's payoff involved in playing the role of the victim and will begin doing things to elicit villain behavior from his older sibling.

2. The older brother will begin coming to you more and more with complaints about his younger brother.

In other words, this is hardly a perfect solution to this problem.

There isn't one, in fact. You're trading one risk (the older brother will continue to hurt the younger brother, and a pattern of abuse will develop in the relationship) for another (1 and 2 above). In the answer to the next question, I describe another approach to the same sort of problem.

Q: **Can you please explain the difference between treating children fairly and treating them the same or equally? Or is there a difference? The kids in question are siblings, ages five and six.**

A: Good question, if for no reason other than this particular topic confuses adults and children alike.

To begin with the obvious, children think the two terms are synonymous. Well, that's not exactly true. Because children are naturally self-centered, the child who complains of being treated "unfairly" really means, more often than not, that he or she has not been given the greater portion or put at the head of the line, or both.

Treating children equally means treating them in exactly the same manner regardless of any quantifiable differences between them. Treating children fairly means treating them with consideration of those differences. Take bedtime, for example, as regards two siblings, ages five and ten. To treat them equally, one would send them to bed at the same time. To treat them fairly, one would let the older one stay up later. Obviously, the younger one wants to be treated equally, while the older one wants to be treated fairly, and rightly so.

Q: **My two daughters, ages five and nine, are generally quite good about playing together and sharing their toys; however, it is almost inevitable that when one of them, using the other's things (with permission), has a game set up (with dolls or what have you) the other one suddenly and inexplicably wants her things back. At this point chaos and anger ensue, and this issue causes major daily discord. I**

don't know how to solve it except by not allowing them to share, but that doesn't seem right.

A: I have a relatively simple solution that will require two kitchen timers and one pad of paper, an investment of less than fifteen dollars.

When one of the kids lets the other play with a toy, the owner must let you know. You tear a slip of paper off the pad, write down the name of the toy, set that child's timer to ring in one hour (an arbitrary time period which should be determined situation by situation), and put the timer on top of the slip of paper. The rule becomes: when the timer rings, the owner can either renew the "lease" or ask that the toy be returned, but not before. If the owner forgets to inform you that she has shared a toy, and an argument begins, then the toy lease begins at the moment you become aware of the loan.

This will involve some conscientious administration on your part, but that will amount to far less hassle than you are currently experiencing. Furthermore, as time goes on, you'll begin to notice that the girls no longer let you know when toys are on loan, but that arguments are no longer occurring. They just need to get over a "hump," and this simple management device will accomplish just that.

DEFIANCE

Defiance is the stock-in-trade of the toddler. Once upon a time, it was nipped in the bud by parents who thought, properly, that if a certain behavior shouldn't be tolerated in adults, it shouldn't be tolerated in children either—a very sensible point of view that resulted in children becoming adults much sooner than are today's children, by and large. Because defiance is not being nipped in the bud as reliably these days, it is not unusual to find it in full bloom in children who have passed their third birthdays (the traditional end of toddlerhood or the "terrible" twos), but don't act like it.

The mother of a four-year-old girl told me that whenever she instructed her daughter to dress for school, the child replied, with defiance dripping from every syllable, "I don't want to, and I'm not going to!" Mom would then tell her that if she didn't dress, and quick, she would go to school in her pajamas. The child would dress. And that was the end of it. Or was it?

"Did I do the right thing?" the mom inquired.

"Does she defy you about other things?"

"Oh," Mom replied, "all the time."

"Then in this case you achieved a short-term objective—she got dressed," I answered, "but you made no progress as regards the real problem."

"What's the real problem?" Mom asked.

The real problem was this little girl's constant defiance of her mother's authority. As was the case over getting dressed for school, Mom would win the occasional skirmish, but the war went on. And it would continue to go on and on and on until Mom "nuked" this little girl and put an end to the war, once and for all.

The problem is, the longer a war of this sort goes on, the worse it's going to get. A four-year-old who has the nerve to tell her mother she's not going to dress for school may well become a thirteen-year-old who tells her mother to go jump in a lake and take a deep breath. This needs to be stopped—not for Mom's betterment, mind you, but for the child's. Research into parenting outcomes is clear that the best-behaved children are also the happiest, most well-adjusted children. The research also tells us that the happiest, most well-adjusted kids have parents who love them without conditions and discipline them with power and purpose. The reason, then, that children should be well disciplined, and therefore well behaved, is not because it's easier to raise a well-behaved child (although it certainly is). The reason is that it is in the child's best interest, both in the short and long haul, to be well behaved.

Before I tell you what I recommended to this four-year-old's mom, I want to be clear on one thing: she handled the immediate situation in a right and proper fashion. To that point, Mom and I are on the same page. If need be, I'd have put said child and her clothes in the backseat of the car and set off for school, telling her that whether she was clothed or not, when we arrived at school, she was going in if I had to carry her in.

But instead of fighting this same battle day in and day out as the mother was doing, I'd have nipped it in the bloom. When the Princess of Petulance arrived home from school that afternoon, I would have told her that as a result of her defiance that morning, she was going to spend the remainder of the day in her room and go to bed immediately after dinner.

And I would have looked her in the eye and said, "And this is the way it's going to be, my love. When you defy me, it will not matter whether you ultimately do what I tell you to do or not. You will be punished."

This little girl needs to know, as do many American children, that obedience is more than simply doing what one is told; it is doing what one is told without even the slightest display of defiance. Some people think this is too much to ask of a child, especially a child as young as four. Not so. We know that most children born before 1960 were obedient by age three. Even today, in underdeveloped countries that have not imported the psychological parenting practices, children are obedient by age three.

In most cases, I recommend Tickets, Strikes, or Charts with defiant children three and older. The Target Misbehavior List should define the form the child's defiance takes. Some kids are passive rebels—they ignore, dawdle, act helpless, whine, and the like. Some rebels are "in your face"—they say things like "I don't have to," "I don't feel like it right now," "Do it yourself," or just plain, "No." In either case, the Target Misbehavior List should be specific. Whether you choose Tickets, Strikes, or Charts is a matter of personal preference. In any case, remember that the Referee's Rule is the key to success. If your child defies you and you respond with "Do you want me to take a ticket?" or, "Did you hear me?" or, "If you don't stop that, I'm going to take a ticket!" you've blown it, and you need to start reading this book again, from page one. You missed something along the way.

Defiant at Home and School

The Daily Report Card system (see pages 89–94) has proven to be very effective in dealing with children whose behavior is a serious problem both at home and at school. I once worked with the parents of a six-year-old boy who was about as defiant a child as I've ever heard of. Mikey was bound and determined to prove that no one—his parents or his teachers—could tell him what to do. His parents were at their wit's end. As they described their travails with Mikey, I could tell they were trying very, very hard not to disturb his self-esteem. This had been their goal, in fact, since day one.

Mikey's parents had tried unsuccessfully for years to have a child. Suddenly, they became pregnant. By the time Mikey was born, he was already an American Idol in their eyes. His parents' worshipful attitude toward him only increased as he grew through infancy and into toddlerhood. Sometime around his second birthday, Mikey the Wonder Child, the Cutest Little Darling Child Ever to Grace Planet Earth, His Most Honored Eminence, suddenly mutated into Mikey the Malevolent, the horror child no one wanted to be around. In subsequent years, he was expelled from two preschool programs for defiance, tantrums, and biting.

Not surprisingly, Mikey was identified as a major behavior problem in kindergarten. Less than a month into the school year, his teacher and the school counselor began suggesting that perhaps a drug would help Mikey sit still and pay attention. His parents came to see me in the spring, hoping I could offer an alternative.

From that point until the end of school, I simply gathered information from the school and coached Mikey's parents on the use of Alpha Speech. As soon as the summer break began, I had them kick Mikey out of the Garden of Eden and start him on Tickets. Mikey started every day with five tickets, which he lost for ignoring his parents, refusing to do what he was told, and yelling at his parents (when they refused to obey him). When he lost his fifth ticket of the day, he was confined to his very boring room and put to bed immediately after supper.

It was a hard slog with Mikey, but I have to hand it to his parents. They followed my instructions, hung in there, and did the hard work. Mikey spent lots of days in his room, but by the time August rolled around, he was a much-improved kid, at which point he began getting his "stuff" back. When he finally figured out that his old ways were not going to work any longer, he began to not just curb his insolence and his outbursts but also to ask for chores to do. He had started the summer with five tickets per day and had worked himself down to three. I thought it was time to tackle the issue of school again. The problem was that the good folks at his previous school were convinced Mikey had a disorder and needed medication. Rather than fight an uphill (and possibly no-win) battle concerning that issue, I had Mikey's parents enroll him in a small Christian school that promised to work with the family.

From day one of the school year, Mikey was on a six-block Daily Report Card. At school, his teacher crossed off blocks for specific misbehaviors. His parents continued the program at home. As was to be expected, Mikey tested his first-grade teacher's mettle, but she passed the test with flying colors. Within less than a month, an outside observer wouldn't have been able to tell that Mikey had once been "the Malevolent." And everyone lived happily ever after.

Defiant at School

The combination of "therapies" that I recommended for Mikey— kicking the child out of the Garden of Eden and then putting him on Tickets, Strikes, Charts, or Daily Report Cards—is my standard approach to defiance. It's a very powerful way of activating the Agony and Godfather Principles and generally brings the child's rebelliousness under control fairly quickly.

A single mother who became familiar with my work, primarily through the members' side of my Web site, related that her son—in the fifth grade at the time she told me this story—had been a major behavior problem in the classroom (but not at home, which is somewhat unusual) since kindergarten. He'd been *the* major problem in every grade, in fact.

Thankfully, she had resisted the school's attempts to get him tested and put on medication. One day, she went to my Web site and happened to find my recommendation—Exile from the Garden—concerning a child who sounded a lot like her son. The problem, however, was that she had no place to store her son's belongings and couldn't afford the monthly charge of a storage locker. She pondered this for a while and came up with a most creative solution.

The next day, when her son went to school, she stayed home. A neighbor helped her install a keyed dead bolt on her son's bedroom door. When he came home and discovered that he couldn't get into his room, he freaked. His room was his Personal Paradise. It contained a television, video game, stereo, computer, slot car racing set, sports equipment, and numerous other things he'd received, mostly from his father and grandparents.

His mother calmly told him that when he had solved his classroom behavior problems to the point that there were no incidents for a month, he would be allowed back in his room. Until then, he was sleeping on the sofa in the living room. In the morning, she would let him into his room to pick out his clothes for school.

He threatened to call the child abuse authority. Mom told him that he was free to do so. He backed down. Then he began to plead and promise. When that didn't work, he began to cry. When that didn't work, he threatened to go live with his father. When that didn't work, he just sat and sulked.

Every Friday he had to take a Weekly Report Card around to his teachers. The Statement of Achievement read: "Xavier behaved himself appropriately in class this week; there were no incidents." His mother told him that he had to obtain all four signatures every week for four weeks running before she would unlock his door.

Six weeks later, she unlocked his door. I heard from her a couple of months later. She told me that Xavier now knows she means business.

"He's a much happier child these days," she wrote.

Fancy that.

Q: We have two children, ages three and four. Recently they've been acting very badly with adult babysitters. How should we handle it when we come home and discover the kids have given a sitter a problem?

A: Here's what you do: hire a babysitter to mind the children one evening, but don't plan on venturing far from home. You should be able to stop what you're doing immediately to come home. Before the sitter arrives, fill her in on what to expect and instruct her to call you on your cell phone *the very moment* a problem begins to occur. (Needless to say, don't tell the kids about this conspiracy.) When you get the call, come home, and put them to bed immediately. (If only one is the problem, however, then only that one is punished.) You should go out early in the evening—five thirty perhaps—so that early bedtime is a *huge deal.* The next morning, tell your kids that the next time they misbehave when a sitter is there, the same thing will happen, but they will also stay in their rooms all day the next day.

A few days later, hire a sitter again—preferably a different one—and have the same preliminary conference. When she comes, sit down with the children and the sitter and have a relatively brief talk. Remind them of what happened the week before and ask, "Are we going to have to come home early again?" The answer, of course, will be a resounding "No!"

Over the next few weeks, go out as often as you can, always having the pre-exit conversation I just described. From that point, when a babysitter is about to arrive, all you will need to do is ask the aforesaid question to ensure that your kids will keep their other personalities under control.

Q: Our three-and-a-half-year-old son is in a mornings-only preschool where he has major "meltdowns" throughout the day. His teacher says he is too disruptive and loud to put him in time-out, so one of the teachers takes him outside and sits with him for a while. He simply doesn't get away with such behavior at home and doesn't even try it. With a new school year just starting, I want to nip this in the bud. So when we got home, I put him in time-out (in a chair in a corner of a room) for an hour. I explained to him that it was because of his fussiness at school. Was I right to put him in such a long time-out?

A: No doubt some people will cringe in horror at the idea of making a three-year-old sit in a chair for an hour, but believe me, that will do no harm. Keep in mind that for a consequence to have a lasting effect, it must result in the formation of a long-term memory. The more memorable the consequence, the more powerful the disciplinary message.

I recommend that you and your son's teachers "double team" him when he throws a classroom tantrum. His teachers should *not* try to calm him down. (They should most definitely not take him outside and sit with him.) Instead, as soon as a tantrum begins, they should remove him from class and call you. You should go to the school as soon as possible and retrieve him. Take him home and put him in his room for the rest of the day and to bed immediately after supper. (Before you begin this rehabilitation program, you might want to consider performing a mild "sterilization" procedure on your son's room, removing and putting away his favorite playthings.)

Long confinement to a relatively boring room will create a much more powerful long-term memory than will an hour in a chair. Regardless, keep in mind that "the third time is the charm." By that, I don't mean that three applications of a consequence should be sufficient to "cure" the problem, but most consequences don't "take" until they've been applied at least three times.

Q: **Our twelve-year-old son and nine-year-old daughter share pet duty in the evenings. Every night we have to remind them, and they always put up a fight before the jobs get done. The chores are definitely not too strenuous for them, and my husband and I feel the responsibility is good for them. The kids know their chores need to be done every night and that they have to do them, yet they mess around until we start nagging; then they blow up. We are tired of all this. Help!**

A: The treatment plan is very specific: First, stop nagging (pestering). Tell the children something along these lines: "You will never, ever again hear either of us so much as even refer to your chores. You know what they are, and we expect you to start them no later than [say] seven o'clock. If you have not started your chores by seven, we will do them for you. Sound good?" Say no more! To any questions, reply, "That's really all we have to say." Then, just sit back and wait.

The next time the kids let the designated "start-time" lapse, just pick yourselves up and go outside and start doing their chores. When you have finished, come inside and announce that it's time for them to go to bed. Be cheery! When they protest that bedtime is at least two hours away, say, "Oh, didn't we tell you? At seven o'clock, either you are on your way out the door to do your chores, or we are out the door to do them for you. If we do them, you have to go to bed as soon as we finish. In fact, if we put even one foot outside to do them, your opportunity has passed, so you might as well be in bed, lights out, by the time we come back. Oh, and by the way, if we do your chores on more than one night, Sunday through Friday, then all weekend privileges for you are cancelled. Any questions?" All of this should be communicated in a matter-of-fact and therefore infuriating tone of voice, accompanied by dumb looks and many shrugs of your shoulders, as if to say "Gosh, kids, we're real, real sorry about all this."

This will activate the Agony Principle (see page 41). The person or persons who become upset over a particular problem will try to solve it. In this case, you are trying to solve a problem—and driving yourselves slowly nuts in the process—that *only* your children can solve. They will solve it when you cause them to begin going nuts because of it.

Now, sit back, relax, and let 'em begin learning how the real world deals with people who do not accept their responsibilities. They're nine and twelve? Good—then it's not too late, but time's a-wastin'!

TANTRUMS

An Atlanta pediatrician sent me an article from the February 2008 issue of *Pediatric News* describing research recently conducted concerning tantrums in children ages three through six. After studying 279 children, the researchers concluded that tantrums in preschool-age kids may be indicative of fairly serious psychological disturbances, including depression and behavior disorders. Nearly half of the kids were so judged, in fact. But what exactly does that mean? Does it mean they have something wrong with them, a neurological abnormality perhaps? That conclusion would follow from what's known as the disease model of mental illness, a model that is used these days to justify the increasingly common practice of giving preschool children psychotropic drugs.

Another point of view is that tantrums beyond the third birthday say more about the parents than the child. In that regard, from all that I gather reading historical writings on children and talking with parents who did most of their child rearing before the psychological parenting revolution of the late 1960s/early 1970s, tantrums beyond the third birthday were a rarity two generations and more ago. Among the American Amish—who adhere to a traditional parenting ethic—that's true even today.

Thirty or so years ago, child psychologist and author (*The First Three Years of Life*) Burton White said that tantrums beyond the second birthday should not be allowed.[1] (I am slightly more tolerant.) He didn't define the exact nature of said intolerance, perhaps because he felt that parents had enough common sense to figure such things out on their own. But common sense has since drowned in a tsunami of psychobabble. It's no longer unusual for children as old as six to still be acting like little lunatics when they don't get their way—thus, the study.

The history of this phenomenon, as anecdotal as it is, strongly suggests that things began to go wrong when American parents stopped listening to their elders and began taking their marching orders from professional experts (yes, like me). Up until then, children were generally cherished, but adults were the center of the American family. Today, children are generally worshipped by parents who face the center rather than occupy it. Kings, queens, demigods, and dictators have always been given to tantrums. Today, the Emperor/Empress wears Pull-ups.

Needless to say, the longer tantrums are allowed, the more habitual and the worse they will become. And equally needless to say, children who throw tantrums on a regular basis are not happy campers. This is indeed a mental health issue, but there is no compelling evidence to date that bad brains are the problem.

Intolerance does not require great drama. In fact, it is best conveyed calmly, with little fanfare. Intolerance begins with never, under any circumstances, giving in to a tantrum, even if one realizes that the precipitating decision was a bit hasty. "Ignore them" is fine advice, but it does not take into account that tantrums have a tendency to follow parents from room to room, escalating in the process. For that reason, I generally advise assigning tantrums to a designated "tantrum place"—some relatively isolated area of the house where rages can be contained until they burn themselves out. Absent a more creative location, the child's room will do. In any case, a sturdy gate may be necessary to persuade the child of the need to stay put.

Obviously, sturdy gates will not contain most five-year-olds, which is why tantrums should not be tolerated beyond the third birthday.

Amy Takes a Powder

Sometime around her third birthday, my daughter Amy (aka Princess Bucket-of-Sass) began throwing wild tantrums when she didn't get her way. As I recall, they began at the dinner table over the issue of green things on her plate. It was our policy that our children were served what everyone else was eating. So if Willie fixed broccoli for dinner, broccoli was on everyone's plate. Amy would pick up the broccoli, piece by piece, and pile it to the side of her plate, on the table. I would reach over and put the broccoli on her plate, at which she would remind me, in a loud voice, that she did not tolerate green things on her plate. I told her in no uncertain terms that I didn't care what her favorite and least-favorite food colors were; if broccoli was being served, it would be served to her.

She would then begin to scream as if she were being dragged unwillingly through some scary "fun" house at Halloween. Once, she pushed herself back from the table. Her chair fell over backward, the inertia of which forced her to do a back flip out of the chair, thus ending up on her hands and knees, looking around as if to say, "What just happened?" Like a rash, the tantrums spread from the dinner table to nearly every aspect of Amy's life in the family. It was as if she were setting up situations where we would say no or insist upon something, and she would begin to scream.

Finally, late one stormy evening, I went into my parenting laboratory and invented the "tantrum place." The next day, right after breakfast (during which green things are generally not an issue), Willie and I sat down with Amy and told her that since she was now screaming a lot when things did not suit her, and because screaming was a very special thing, we had decided to give her a special place for her special screaming—the downstairs bathroom, otherwise known as a powder room, which was appropriate since from that point on when she threw a tantrum, she "took a powder."

We took her inside the bathroom and pointed out that it was an ideal place for screaming, the most ideal place in the house in fact. It was small, so her screams would be really loud in there. If her screams made her have to use the toilet, it was right there. And if her screams made her need a drink of water, a sink was right there (we provided a special screaming cup for her).

"When we displease you, Amy, and you need to scream, just come in here, close the door, and scream all you want. If you forget to go on your own, we'll put you in here. When you're done screaming, you can come out."

And that was that. When she screamed, she either ran straight to the bathroom and let it all hang out or we took her by the hand and led her—sometimes we had to drag her—there. In fairly short order, Amy's tantrums were under control. Since then, I am told, my invention has been used successfully by hundreds of satisfied parents.

How did people who are now in their eighties and nineties—folks who raised their kids in the pre-psychological era—get their children to stop throwing tantrums by age three? Some tell me they spanked, hard, when the first tantrum occurred (and keep in mind that their kids were toilet-trained before age two, so these spankings were not administered through diapers). Some promptly took their kids to their bedrooms and made them stay a long time, perhaps as long as the rest of the day. A few elderly women have told me that the very first time one of their kids tossed a "hissy," they calmly drew a glass of water and poured it over the child. They then put the glass down and walked away. This is surely biblical, because the first tantrum was the last (Matt. 20:16).

Emma Gets a Grip

Actually, my preferred nomenclature for tantrums is "high self-esteem seizures" (HSES). That's a much more accurate term. A tantrum occurs because the parents are not obeying or properly pleasing the child, at which point the child's high self-esteem begins to spasm. These spasms cause children to scream, cry, and yell things—often incoherent things.

Sometimes, the spasms are so powerful that the child is thrown to the ground, whereupon he begins thrashing about. The loud incoherencies continue and usually become more intense as the HSES grips the child even more violently. If the seizure does not throw the child to the ground, the child may attempt to discharge the pain by grabbing nearby objects and throwing them, or hitting the parents, or even attempting to bite them. Depending on the child's age and history, an HSES can last anywhere from fifteen minutes to several hours.

Such was the case with five-year-old Emma. Her HSESs had been going on since she was three and occurred at least three times daily. Emma's parents had already removed nearly everything from her bedroom except heavy furniture because when she was in the throes of an HSES, she often began throwing anything she could get her hands on. Having read my newspaper column for several years, the parents were somewhat familiar with my philosophy and approach to behavior problems. So when their daughter had one of her frequent seizures, they confined her to her room for the day. The problem was that she would not go to her room without being taken there somewhat forcefully. The further problem was that when her parents tried to take her to her room, she would hit at them, kick at them, scratch them, and even try to bite them. When they finally got her into her room, she would begin kicking the walls and furniture and throwing things. This could go on for several hours. When the HSES burned itself out, Emma's parents let her out of her room.

By the time the parents sought my advice, they were desperate, which was good, because desperate people follow directions very well. Before coming to me, Emma's parents had seen another psychologist who told them their daughter had early-onset bipolar disorder (EOBD) or childhood bipolar disorder. He had informed them—with great solemnity, I'm sure—that EOBD ran in families and involved a rather serious biochemical imbalance (none of which has been proven to be the case with any family or any one). After frightening the parents half to death, he had recommended medication and weekly play therapy sessions for the child with a play therapy specialist, at two hundred dollars a session. Smelling a rat, they passed on the faux diagnosis and came to me.[2]

I told this wild child's parents, "Pick a quiet moment to sit down with your daughter and apologize for the manner in which you've been handling her tantrums."

They looked at one another, incredulous. "Apologize?" they asked.

"Yep," I said. "Apologize. Tell her you spoke with a doctor and he said you should never, ever have tried to force her to go to her room when she has a tantrum. He said she is old enough to go to her room on her own. The doctor said that from now on, when she has an HSES, you are to simply tell her to go to her room and get control of herself. If she obeys, right away, she only has to stay there until she calms down and is ready to come out and apologize to you. If she refuses to go to her room, then you have to take her there. If you have to take her there, she has to stay for the rest of the day and go to bed an hour early.

"Oh," I continued, "and also tell her that this doctor said that until you are able to fix all of the damage to her room, you can't buy her anything other than absolutely necessary things, like food. Also tell her that you're going to talk with the doctor every couple of weeks and do what he tells you to do."

I saw the parents two weeks later. They told me their daughter had thrown one tantrum since the last appointment, a huge change from an average of three or four a day. A month later, they told me they were living with an entirely different child. Not only were the tantrums gone, but they could tell, as could others, that an overall positive change had taken place. Their daughter was generally happier, and they were beginning to say no to her without lots of anxiety because she was now able to accept it.

It's obvious that gene-based biochemical imbalances in the brain cannot be cured in a month simply by telling a child that when she has a tantrum she can either go to her room on her own or be taken there, but regardless, she has to apologize before she can come out. So what's the explanation for wild tantrums of Emma's sort? The explanation is that just as children can develop bad behavioral habits, they can develop bad emotional habits (and they can develop bad mental habits too). In most cases, it's impossible to tell just how the bad habit, whatever the sort, got started. It just did. When it first reared its ugly little head, it threw the parents off balance. Because they responded ineffectively, the problem began to grow. And that's all the explanation necessary. In the final analysis, the pertinent question is not, "Why?" but, "What are we going to do about it?" In most cases, the former question is a distraction. It throws people even further off balance. That's how high self-esteem seizures become "early-onset bipolar disorder."

Q&A

Q: **My three-year-old daughter is having a problem with a much smaller two-year-old she sees often at the park. My daughter will bring along a doll or other toy to play with, but she usually loses interest after a while. At that point, the toddler will start playing with it. Suddenly, my daughter wants it back. If I tell her that she needs to share, she begins a tantrum and we have to leave. Or if I tell the toddler it is time for her to give the toy back to my daughter, the other mother looks at me like I am evil. This is creating a lot of tension for me. What do you suggest?**

A: It seems to me that this problem can be solved by not allowing your daughter to take a toy to the park. Your daughter hasn't learned to share willingly, and two-year-olds are generally incapable of sharing, so the solution is to eliminate the source of the problem—the object to be shared.

Furthermore, instead of waiting until the proverbial iron is hot before you try teaching your daughter the finer points of sharing, role-play various sharing situations with her at home. You play the role of another child and help her develop the skills she needs to play in a give-and-take fashion with other children.

Another solution is to let your daughter take a toy to the park on the condition that she takes another one for the two-year-old and lets her play with it the entire time.

Q: **Our three-year-old son is mostly well behaved; however, when he doesn't get his way or becomes frustrated for whatever reason, he will swat whatever thing (not people) is in his way. Sometimes, when he swats, he will scream something incoherent. If I say, "No!" he will look at me defiantly and do it again. He gets over his little tantrum fairly quickly, but not until he has swatted something and screamed. How should I deal with this? I have tried time-out, and he will stay put for as long as I tell him, but it doesn't really seem to help.**

A: He screams something incoherent, then you shout something, and so on. Sounds like a failure to communicate. Come to think of it, I know some adults who, when frustrated, hit or throw things and yell—no doubt related to unresolved toddler issues.

I recommend that you deal with your son's swatting and incoherent yelling by completely ignoring it. As it stands, he is not hurting anything other than perhaps his hand, but if you continue paying a lot of attention to this, he may soon begin throwing things, breaking things, and even turning his aggressions toward people. Ignored, this too will likely pass. Otherwise, this molehill may quickly grow into a mountain.

Q: **Our middle child, age five, is aggressive, loud, and disrespectful when anyone dares to deny her or make her do something she doesn't want to do. The end result is a tantrum that can last up to an hour. The powder room is her "tantrum place" (we've read your books), but she opens the door and screams down the hall. In desperation, we emptied her room of toys, books, and all but essential clothes. It took her a month to earn her stuff back, at which point she went right back to square one. Last night, she screamed**

in church, the parking lot, and all the way home because we left early to get our littlest to bed, and she didn't get to have a cookie. We're at the end of our rope. Help!

A: You're doing fine. You aren't giving in to her tantrums, which is Tantrum Principle Number One. You've created a "safe" but isolated place in which she can throw tantrums to her heart's content, which is Tantrum Principle Number Two. You followed through on a consequence that would leave a fairly indelible impression on most children her age. Last night, you didn't turn around and retrieve the cookie. Like I said, you're doing fine, but your daughter's rehabilitaiton is going to take some time.

   She's decided that you're not the boss of her, that nothing you can do to her will make a difference, that she is the sole authority in her life, that she is going to have her way come perdition or high water, that no one has the right to tell her what to do, and so on. She's a rebel with a cause, which is to prove that she is a supreme being.

   Some children come into the world determined to prove that they are above any and all law. Current pseudoscientific mythology has it that such children are carriers of a myste-rious chemical imbalance that is triggered by the word *no*. In Germany, the chemical imbalance is triggered by *nein*. In Russia, it is triggered by *nyet*. The more traditional (some would say benighted) view, of which I am a proponent, is that whereas the average child is bad to the muscle, these children are bad to the bone. They need a lot of love and a lot of con-sistent discipline, but they also need parents with a sense of humor. Lacking that quality, they can easily go bonkers.

   Love and a sense of humor are up to you. As for the con-sistent discipline, keep in mind that for your daughter to begin mending her ways, the consequences of her behavior must bother her more than her behavior bothers you. Strip her room again, but this time, tell her that she must go a month without throwing a tantrum in order to get her stuff back, and that any tantrum, however small, during that time starts the month over again. Mind you, it may take her a long time to get her stuff back; ten years maybe. I'm just kidding. If you laughed, then you are on the way to recovery.

REFUSING TO USE THE POTTY

Is it easier to house train a six-month-old puppy or a one-year-old dog? The puppy, right? If you wait until the dog is a year old to begin training, you will have the devil to pay. Furthermore, you may be dealing with a dog who just doesn't seem to "get it" for several years or more. Most people understand that waiting too long to house train a puppy is going to create problems. Why do these same folks not understand that the same applies to a child?

Historical and cross-cultural data clearly indicates that the "season" for toilet training is between fifteen and twenty-four months. The research is unequivocal: the longer one waits after twenty-four months to initiate training, the harder it is likely to be for both parent and child.

In the mid-1950s, Harvard University researchers found that nearly 90 percent of America's children had been successfully trained before they reached their second birthdays. Today, courtesy of several decades of toilet-babble issuing primarily from pediatrician and author T. Berry Brazelton, parents wrongly think training a child under age two is psychologically harmful, if not impossible.

So, they wait. And they wait. And they wait. They're waiting, they tell me, for their children to show some of Brazelton's "readiness signs," which he snatched out of the thinnest of air to make it appear that his "child-centered" (a euphemism for upside-down) recommendations were based on solid science.

Compounding the problem is that, because today's parents believe that toilet training is fraught with apocalyptic psychological pitfalls, they don't *tell* their children to use the toilet. Instead of using Alpha Speech, they use Milquetoast Speech. They cajole, encourage, bribe, bargain, and so on.

"Sweetie, do you want to try to use the big-girl potty today? No? All right then, but when you think you'd like to try, let me know, okay? We have a potty for you that plays your favorite Barney songs, and when you decide to sit on it, we can have a cookie and ice cream party!"

Many, if not most, of the professionals to whom parents look for parenting advice maintain that toilet training below age two requires "force." Wrong again! If a child is not trained during toilet training's appointed season and becomes what is known as "toileting resistant," it will require *force* to accomplish what could have been accomplished months and even, in some cases, *years* before with relative ease.

I'm reserving the subject of how to toilet-train a young toddler (or an older toddler, and even a child who is no longer a toddler) for my next book. For now, I'm only going to tell one story of toilet training catastrophe turned quickly into toilet training success.

"He Just Doesn't Seem to Care!"

A few years ago, while flying from somewhere to somewhere else, my seatmate and I began talking. He asked what I did and I told him, upon which he began sharing with me some of the problems he and his wife were having with their four-year-old son, primary of which was his refusal to use the toilet. Like all too many American children his age, he was still in diapers, and acting as if he just didn't care. Dad asked my advice. I told him that he and his wife should get rid of the diapers, "pull-ups," and any other evidence of the problem—today. The child should walk around the house wearing only thin cotton underpants (not absorbent training pants!) and a T-shirt until his education was complete. Meanwhile, they should pump him full of water. I emphasized water, as opposed to sugar-sweetened drinks, including fruit juice. They should set a timer to go off every hour, on the hour, at which time the child should be directed, or if need be, *taken* to the bathroom and told he cannot come out until he has produced and appropriately deposited a significant amount of waste of one sort or another. Furthermore, I said, accidents should result in the child being sent to his room for the remainder of the day. The room should be "cleansed" of his favorite playthings. He has to wait in his room until the potty bell next rings. In this case, however, when he produces, he goes back to his room until the bell rings again. And so on. The father listened intently, but I couldn't tell whether he thought I was a nut job or truly onto something.

A few months later, he sent me this e-mail: "You may remember sitting next to the dad who complained about his four-year-old son's toileting problems. You were so right about the 'cold turkey' thing. To make a long story short, I spoke to my wife on the phone right after our flight and told her what you had said. That evening, while I was still away, she began the program. When the bell rang, she took him to the bathroom and told him he couldn't come out until he'd done something, and the something had to more than just a 'piddle.' Meanwhile, she was pumping him full of water, as you had advised. She even told him that if he hadn't gone by bedtime, she'd put his sleeping bag in there. It took him four hours of standing in the bathroom with nothing to do before he gave in. Anyway, it worked, and he was incredibly proud of himself. He hasn't had a problem since. Amazing that something we'd struggled with for two years was over with in one night."

Please note, Dear Reader, that the "force" in question did not create a psychological issue; rather, it eliminated one.

CHAPTER FIVE

Seven Tales of the Strange and Unexpected

I never cease to be amazed at the difficulty many mental health professionals have thinking outside the box. That is, they seem unable to think outside of the theoretical frameworks their training fixed around their brains. It seems all that many folks in my profession know to do is diagnose and render cookie-cutter "treatments" that carry the very real potential of solving nothing and even making the problem worse. They certainly waste lots of time, energy, and people's money. Kids do the darnedest things. Not because they have psychological problems, but simply because they are kids. Here are seven prime examples.

HENRY BANGS HIS HEAD

Henry's parents were beside themselves. Their imaginations were running wild. Needless to say, they weren't thinking straight.

At the time, Henry had just turned three. Shortly before his third birthday, he had developed the rather disconcerting habit of violently banging his head on a hard surface, such as the floor, a wall, or a piece of furniture, when his parents didn't give him his way. At first, they thought it was just a stage that would pass quickly if they ignored it. Not so. Over the next few weeks, it got progressively worse. The parents then tried teaching him what they termed "alternative ways of expressing his feelings." That's the way today's parents talk, you know. They tried to teach him to stomp his right foot when he was mad, but he made it clear he preferred head banging to foot stomping. They tried teaching him to shout, "I'm really mad!" and indeed he began shouting, "I'm really mad!" while banging his head. As a result, the suspicious red, black, and blue bruises on his forehead became more and more pronounced. His parents were convinced that it was only a matter of time before a child abuse SWAT team would storm their house in the middle of the night, snatch Henry from his bed, and spirit him off to foster care oblivion.

In desperation, they made an appointment with a child psychologist whom their pediatrician recommended. She told them to ignore it. They said they had. She told them to ignore it some more. At the second appointment, when they told her that ignoring wasn't working, the psychologist suggested Henry was autistic or perhaps bipolar. Oh me!

Meanwhile, smaller and smaller things were triggering head banging episodes, and the bruises were so colorful his parents were rightly afraid to take him out in public. They cancelled their next appointment with Doctor Diagnosem and decided that when one of these episodes started, they would go to Henry and simply try to prevent him from hurting himself further. That benevolent strategy did nothing but provoke even more rage, however. As the parents struggled with Henry to keep him from banging his head, he would bite and scratch at them.

Note how downright bad the psychologist's advice had been. How, pray tell, does a parent ignore it when his or her just-turned-three-year-old darling is beating huge, swelling bruises on his forehead several times a day? I'll bet the psychologist wouldn't have been able to "just ignore it" if the head banger were hers. Besides, that sort of cavalier advice downright ignores the parents' emotional plight. Never in their lives had they felt more anxiety, more of a sense of helplessness and failure, and yet some high-minded professional is telling them to just ignore their son's self-destructive episodes!

The first thing I told them was that they could no more prevent Henry from banging his head than they could prevent him from throwing any other form of a tantrum. If he wanted to throw a fit, he was going to, and if he wanted to bang his head, he was going to. Their attempts to prevent him from banging required constant vigilance, something they weren't capable of sustaining. They could have him wear a football helmet with a childproof chin strap, but that would probably enrage him further.

I said, "The more anxious you are and the harder you try to stop him from banging his head, the more determined to bang he's going to become." They regarded me with the most crestfallen looks I'd seen in a long time, so I quickly continued: "Toddlers have a reputation for reacting to frustration by doing bizarre things like banging their heads, biting themselves, and pulling out their hair—the kind of aberrant behavior we associate with the inmates of an eighteenth-century asylum. As loony as this sort of stuff seems, it's not all that unusual."

Indeed, toddlers bang heads and bite themselves and throw themselves around because they're uncivilized and can't handle the word *no*. They continue to hurt themselves because they get attention for it. The trick, then, was to come up with a way of not giving Henry attention for head banging without, however, ignoring it.

There is a way of doing just that. I've recommended it many times and have never once heard of it failing. Here's a step-by-step of what I told Henry's parents to do:

1. Find a section of blank wall in some relatively out-of-the-way, yet accessible, part of the house.
2. Using a stud-finder, locate the vertical studs.
3. Using a washable crayon, draw a two-foot diameter circle on the wall, between the studs, positioning the center at the same height as Henry's forehead.

4. Take Henry to the circle and say, "This is your new and very special head-banging place. It's the best place in the whole house for banging your head. From now on, when you want to bang your head, just come over here and bang it right in the circle (pointing to its center). Like this!" (I told Henry's father to get down on his knees and bang his head a few times in the circle.)

5. Tell Henry how good it felt to bang your head in that particular spot and encourage him to try it for himself.

Since Henry's parents had also been teaching him to stomp his feet, I suggested (with only part of my tongue in my cheek) that they also draw a circle on the floor, directly beneath the head-banging circle and tell Henry it was his very own special foot-stomping place. He could now stand in one place and bang his head and stomp his foot at the same time, which was bound to help his coordination, if nothing else.

"Anyhow," I said, "Henry's gonna look at you like you've lost your marbles. The next time he begins throwing a tantrum, I guarantee he'll start banging his head on whatever's convenient. In that event, quickly pick him up—or drag him, as the case may be—and take him to the circle on the wall and say, 'No, no, no. Bang your head here, in your special place!' and walk away."

I assured them that if they did this every time the head-banging started, they should notice it begin to taper off in about a week, at the latest. After all, there's no future in head banging unless someone gets all bent out of shape about it.

Within four days, Henry's head banging stopped and his bruises began to fade. Best of all, his bipolar disorder with autistic features went into remission and stayed there.

MEGAN YANKS HER HAIR OUT BY THE HANDFULS

The parents of a four-year-old girl named Megan asked for my thoughts on why their daughter was pulling out her own hair and what they should do about it. The hair pulling had suddenly and mysteriously started six months before and was producing huge bald spots on Megan's otherwise pretty head.

The parents first sought the advice of a therapist who told them Megan was stressed-out over the impending birth of a sibling. How he came to this rather odd conclusion is anyone's best guess. Meanwhile, Megan's hair pulling got progressively worse. After four months the parents stopped the therapy, after which there was serious question as to who was pulling out more hair, Megan or her parents.

Quite obviously, by yanking bald spots in her head, Megan was able to be the center of attention in the family. Someone might ask why a child would be willing to endure such discomfort, even pain, just to get something she was getting enough of already. The answer is quite simple: children are irrational. Megan wasn't being manipulative. She wasn't thinking this through; she was simply doing what comes naturally to children: whatever it takes to be at the center of a cyclone.

I told Megan's parents that there was no way of making a definitive connection between their daughter's hair pulling and the new sibling—this was pure speculation. Furthermore, it was speculation of the sort that, even if true, was fairly worthless. What were the parents to do? Postpone the second child's arrival?

Psychological explanations of misbehavior—and make no mistake about it, this child's hair pulling was most definitely a misbehavior—often have the unintended effect of paralyzing the parents' authority. As a consequence, they start walking on proverbial tiptoes around the child. When a child senses a vacuum of authority, the child's problems, whatever their source, will surely worsen.

With Henry's head-banging place in mind (see previous section), I advised Megan's parents to tell their daughter that she could only pull her hair in the downstairs bathroom; that it was her new "hair-pulling place."

If she pulled her hair elsewhere, they would put her in the bathroom and require her to stay for at least ten minutes, with instruction to pull to her heart's content. Meanwhile, the parents had to stop mentioning Megan's hair in any context, a prohibition that even extended to praising her for not pulling.

The next day, Megan's mom sent me the following e-mail:

> When she began pulling her hair during lunch today, I calmly led her to the bathroom. I told her that this was the new hair-pulling place, the only place where she could pull her hair, and to go right ahead and pull as much as she wanted.
>
> "Will you watch?" she asked. I told her no, shut the door, and returned to the table. Fifteen minutes later, she came out and finished her lunch. Her dad is reading to her as I type this, and we have not made one mention of hair all evening. I can't say that she is cured, but being in the bathroom just that once and my not flipping out about it seems to be helping already. This has been the calmest evening we've had in half a year.

Over the next couple of weeks, Megan pulled her hair only around people whom she thought would give her attention for it, like her grandparents. On each occasion, her parents simply put her in the bathroom and encouraged her to pull, pull, and pull some more. On none of these occasions did Megan stay in the bathroom for more than a few minutes and always emerged with no sign of having pulled at all!

Decades ago, this sort of approach to a disciplinary issue was called "reverse psychology." Just goes to show: there is nothing new under the sun.

Things Get "Tricky"

Ah, but our story does not end there. Shortly after I published Megan's hair-pulling story in my nationally syndicated newspaper column, the executive director of the Trichotillomania Learning Center, Inc. sent me a letter accusing me of dispensing harmful, misleading information and said that sending the little girl to the bathroom to pull her hair amounted to "shaming." She also chastised me for not even mentioning "the name of the disorder, trichotillomania."

On their Web site (www.trich.org), TLC identifies *trichotillomania* (TTM) as compulsive hair-pulling, an impulse-control disorder that seems to "strike most frequently in the pre- or early-adolescent years." Treatments listed on the Web site include both psychological and pharmaceutical approaches.

In the first place, there is no objective scientific evidence that pulling out one's own hair, no matter how often or how much, qualifies as a "disorder." Second, genuine disorders do not disappear in response to calm, authoritative instruction. Since Megan stopped her hair-pulling after being told to pull in the bathroom only, she clearly didn't have a disorder. She "had" nothing, in fact, but was surely developing a habit that conceivably could have developed into a compulsion and that might have eventually resulted in a diagnosis.

A year later, the parents wrote me the following: "Megan is a much happier little girl these days, not to mention that our family is much calmer. She even laughs about it now. One day, she put her hand up to scratch her head and said, 'Don't worry, Mom, I'm not pulling my hair out, I'm just scratching an itch.'"

So much for TLC's assertion that my recommendation amounted to "shaming": how, pray tell, is being told that you can pull all the hair you want, as long as you pull in the bathroom, going to cause shame? Being permitted to do something within certain benign boundaries is not shameful. It is liberating. In this case, it liberated Megan from the habit of hair pulling.

Unfortunately, it is certainly the case that too many parents of hair-pulling children do try to shame or scare their kids into stopping by telling them how awful they look, spanking them, telling them their hair will never grow back, and so on. It is axiomatic that shaming a person who is engaging in compulsive behavior will only exacerbate the problem. But as this case illustrates, shame is not the only alternative to professional treatment.

As I told TLC's director, "a bad habit does not a disorder make."

Nonetheless, one must wonder how many "disorders" have been manufactured out of nothing more.

Three years later, Megan's mom wrote me again, and again the news was nothing but good.

"Megan is doing fantastically and never did go back to pulling her hair. I saw that TLC took you to task for not considering that she had trichotillomania. She had a bad case of wanting to be the center of attention is all! She is so smart and funny and is a really sweet child. I hate to think what may have been the case if we had continued with the therapist or consulted TLC."

My final word on the subject: sometimes, with the best of intentions, mental health professionals do more harm than good. I think it is nothing short of tragic that American parents are seeking professional help for child-rearing problems in greater and greater numbers every year, *which is not to say that professional help is never warranted*. I am convinced, however, that the overwhelming majority of the problems in question could have been resolved, as was the case here, with proper use of some good, old-fashioned, creative discipline.

ROBERTA WON'T "UNBOND" WITH HER FOOD

Six-year-old Roberta would suddenly decide, during a family meal, that she could not swallow her food. The food in question might even have been her favorite food.

"When I tell her she can't spit it out," her mother told me, "she will defy the laws of physics and hold the bite in her mouth for hours. No kidding! She once held a bite for four hours."

Roberta's parents had tried everything. They had required her to remain at the table until she swallowed, in response to which she would sit, obediently, for hours. They had tried returning her unfinished food to her at the next meal, removing toys and privileges for up to weeks at a time, banishment to her room without toys, spanking, praising when she swallowed, and withholding dessert. Nothing had worked. They were desperate.

"Help us!" they wailed.

Oh, I neglected to mention, Roberta had been adopted internationally. The parents were convinced there was some arcane connection between adoption and not swallowing food. So the first thing I did was to assure them that Roberta's "issue" was not even remotely related to being adopted. This was just one of those weird, strange, inexplicable things that some children sometimes do, for no obvious reason at all. The fact is—and I hope a lot of adoptive parents are reading this— lots of children do odd things. In fact, nearly every child acquires some "oddity" at some point or another; it sticks around for a while, and then the child drops it.

Today's adoptive parents are conditioned and even brainwashed into thinking that every slightly out-of-the-ordinary thing their adopted children do is related in some Freudian manner to adoption. In this regard, the terms "abandonment issues" and "bonding problems" are flung about recklessly in the adoption community as if they are one-size-fits-all explanations.

Dr. Psychobabble: "Mr. and Mrs. Schmeegle, my exhaustive (and expensive) battery of (meaningless) tests reveals that your daughter refuses to swallow because swallowing her food is equivalent, in her subconscious, with abandonment. At some point during a meal, she imagines that a bite of food is herself, and she cannot swallow because to swallow is to abandon herself. In effect, she is bonding with her food as a means of compensating for the bonding disruption caused by the adoption. Very simple, really."

Think long and hard about the following question: if a child does something odd and the child was *not* adopted, is the child doing the odd thing in question because she's having non-adoption or non-abandonment issues? The answer, of course, is no. My point is that some of the things children do defy explanation.

Furthermore, some, if not most, of the odd stuff in question is harmless to the point of being funny. What Roberta was doing was funny (to me, at least), but it was also a very clever, subtle form of defiance. The more subtle the defiance, the more intelligent the child (good news, eh?), and, in turn, the more creative the discipline must be.

The cure to Roberta's "International Adoption Manufactured Swallowing Abandonment Disorder" (IAMSAD) involved my good friend, the Doctor. I told Roberta's parents to tell their slyly defiant and highly intelligent little princess that they had called the Doctor, and he said that not being able to swallow happens because a child is tired and doesn't even know it.

As in, "Your doctor said that from now on, if you take a bite and you are so tired that you can't swallow, you have to go to the bathroom, spit it out, and go to bed."

And that was that. Roberta's bad case of IAMSAD cleared up immediately. Funny how the threat of early bedtime will resolve deep-seated adoption issues.

SAMMY SCRATCHES HIMSELF

My creation, the Doctor, made another curative appearance in the case of Sammy, a five-year-old boy who had taken to scratching his arms and legs until they bled. He claimed they itched, but his pediatrician ruled out any skin conditions. Sammy's mother told me that he would get her attention by breaking open a self-inflicted wound that was beginning to heal and then showing it to her. She had tried everything from casually telling him to wash and bandage his wounds to scolding him. Nothing had worked, and she was, she said, "at wit's end."

It seemed like a perfect fit for my imaginary friend, so I told Mom to sit Sammy down when the proverbial iron was cold—in other words, when a scratching incident had not recently happened—and tell him, with great solemnity, that she had spoken to the Doctor about his scratching. He had said that when a child scratches himself a lot, and especially when he often makes himself bleed, it means he's not getting enough sleep.

The prescription: For the next two weeks, and maybe longer if he was still scratching, Sammy had to go to bed right after supper—in bed, curtains drawn, lights out. In addition, every time he scratched himself, he had to go to his room and lie down, curtains drawn, for an hour.

Even if the scratching stopped before two weeks was up, he had to go to bed right after supper for the full "treatment" period, at which time Mom would give the Doctor a progress report. I told her to tell Sammy that she truly hoped he would only have an early bedtime for two weeks, but that it all depended on the Doctor's judgment.

This approach accomplishes several things: First, it redefines the problem. Scratching is replaced by lack of sleep as the primary issue. Second, the gain of being able to get attention by scratching is hopefully outweighed by the desire to restore normal bedtime. Third, authority over the issue is assigned to a dispassionate third party, thus effectively neutralizing the emotions that have become attached to and are fueling the scratching.

I was, by the way, fully prepared to recommend that this mom ask Sammy's real-life doctor for a referral to a therapist in their area with a good track record when it comes to working with children, but my prediction was that after two weeks of early bedtime, this little fellow would be itching to have his normal bedtime restored.

And that is precisely what happened. A month later, Mom wrote: "We took action the day we heard back from you and it worked! He had a couple of relapses early on, but we simply sent him to his room to lie down for an hour, as the Doctor prescribed. At this point, his skin is healing well."

That Doctor—what a guy!

SONNY WON'T POOP WITHOUT A PULL-UP

The parents of a six-year-old boy e-mailed me in desperation. Sonny absolutely refused to use the toilet for bowel movements. He would only poop in a pull-up and if his parents refused to give him one, he would hold for days. Finally, afraid of the medical consequences of his holding, they would relent and put one on him. Sonny would then go off in the house somewhere, squat, and poop. His parents would then help him clean himself. A doctor had found no physical problem, they said. I could have told them that. Quite obviously, Sonny had complete control of his bowel movements.

I began my reply by asking, rhetorically, "Who gives Sonny that most nefarious of devices, the greatest toilet-training scam of all time, a Pull-up? Answer: You do. Inescapable conclusion: as long as you provide this counterproductive alternative, he has no reason to use the toilet.

"You've told me enough to know that Sonny's poopiness is most definitely within his control. He does not have 'on purposes' (they do not qualify as 'accidents') at school, and his bowel movements do not suddenly explode from his body to his shock and surprise. He tells you he needs a Pull-up, you give him one, and then he goes off somewhere and poops. Then *you* change him and help him clean himself. The last time I checked, that qualified as Olympic-class *enabling*.

"In pediatric parlance, your Sonny's problem is known as 'stool refusal,' the incidence of which has increased dramatically as the average age of toilet training has increased well beyond twenty-four months. The problem is rarely seen in children who are toilet trained before their second birthdays. I also suspect that some of the increase is due to the fact that whereas pre-1960s parents usually bowel trained before bladder training, modern parents have reversed that sequence.

"In any case, and as you might well imagine, as the frequency of stool withholding has increased, so has my experience with it. The solution is really quite simple: Tell Sonny, today, that you have decided he can no longer poop in "pull-ups," period. Throw them away! Furthermore, if he soils his clothes, he has to hand wash them himself (first 'dunking' them in the toilet and then finishing the process in a large bucket that you place in the bathroom) until they are clean enough to wear again. Make it very clear that you will *under no circumstances* put soiled clothing in the washing machine. After he finishes washing out his clothes, he spends the remainder of the day in his room (the 'entertainment value' of which you should reduce significantly) and goes to bed early."

Before Sonny's rehabilitation program began, his bedroom was stripped down to bare essentials—no toys, no games, no electronics of any sort.

I heard nothing from the parents for three suspense-filled weeks. Finally, this e-mail from Sonny's mother: "Sorry to take so long getting back to you, John. To be honest, we were waiting to make sure the cure was for real. The first day of the new program, a Saturday, after we took away the "pull-ups," Sonny had an on-purpose in his clothes at ten o'clock in the morning. We had him hand wash the soiled articles. We then confined him to his room for the rest of the day and put him to bed right after supper. He has not had a problem since. It took us three weeks to accept that, after more than three years of battles, the problem was really over and done with."

This story simply illustrates, once again, the curative power of the Agony Principle. For three years, these *parents* had been in agony over their son's poopy problem. When they transferred that agony to their son by simply making him an offer he couldn't refuse (the Godfather Principle), he saw the wisdom of getting his act together and growing up.

This stuff is not complicated, folks!

RAFAEL STEALS FOOD AND HIDES IT

Seven-year-old Rafael had already been tagged with two fake disorders—attention-deficit hyperactivity disorder and oppositional defiant disorder—for which he was taking medication. He didn't need another diagnosis, for sure. His problem was that he took food—eggs, fruit roll-ups, cake mixes, and so on—out of the kitchen and hid them in his bedroom and bathroom and then pretended to cook with them. His parents installed locks on the bathroom and kitchen cabinets, and when they first consulted me, they were trying to figure out a way to lock the refrigerator.

Rafael's mother said, "When we find one thing, he tells us where other stuff is. He doesn't seem contrite at all. We've taken away privileges, spanked, and sent him to bed early, but nothing seems to work. We even have a door alarm on his room so we'll know if he gets up in the middle of the night, but this doesn't stop him from sneaking food during the day."

The parents wanted to know if there was a way to stop the food stealing, but they also wanted to know if it was symptomatic of a serious mental problem. Indeed, they were describing obsessive behavior, and some other therapist might have diagnosed this little guy with obsessive-compulsive disorder and recommended yet more drugs. I told the parents that despite the symptom picture, I thought Rafael was simply being disobedient and sneaky, which describes lots of kids. Nothing he was doing, however, was destructive, much less self-destructive. Furthermore, he was obviously using the food he stole for creative purposes, but that didn't mean it was okay for him to steal it.

I didn't think this problem was going to yield to standard disciplinary approaches. I did think, however, that it might be possible to channel it such that what was then inappropriate became appropriate.

Rafael's problem had all the characteristics of a game, much like hide-and-seek. As things stood, he controlled the rules. Rafael stole something, hid it, and his parents went on a search to find it. This sounded less like a mental problem than an example of how children figure out how to turn the parent/child relationship upside-down. Mind you, this is less "manipulative" than it is an example of a child's natural, intuitive genius for such things. With all that in mind, I crafted a three-step treatment plan.

Step One: Rafael's parents took all the locks off the cabinets. They hadn't worked and were only making Rafael that much more determined to do his food-stealing thing. Removing the locks disabled a critical element of the food-stealing drama.

Step Two: They told Rafael that they were sorry for reacting to his food taking as if it was something bad. "We realize it's just your way of telling us that you want to learn to cook!" they said, in which case they were going to begin teaching him. In this way, the problem was redefined—it was no longer disobedience; it was creativity!

Step Three: Rafael's parents took him to the store and purchased what he needed to cook several simple meals for the family. (If you're thinking that teaching a boy to cook at age seven is rather odd, remember that the typical American girl of two generations past had started learning to cook before she was seven. And what does gender have to do with it?) With loving patience, they began teaching him how to cook.

It was important that his parents not expect Rafael to stop stealing food all of a sudden. He didn't, in fact. But when he did, they simply showed him how to cook or incorporate into a recipe what he'd stolen. Make every "crime" a learning opportunity, I told them. I emphasized the importance of not saying things like, "When are you going to stop this?" because any display of exasperation on their part would make things worse.

Rafael's parents kept up his cooking lessons. I suggested that when he was a bit older, they might consider enrolling him in cooking classes or find a private cooking tutor for him. When all was said and done, they had taken control of the original problem and transformed the negativity of it into something immensely positive!

This story illustrates the limitations of a straightforward disciplinary approach to misbehavior. When misbehavior is "outside the box," it's generally the case that the solution has to be equally unorthodox.

CHATTY CATHY TELLS EVERYBODY EVERYTHING

Eight-year-old Cathy's mother asked my advice concerning her daughter's often embarrassing tendency to intrude into adult conversations and begin reporting the latest, and often embarrassing, news from her family. Mom had explained to Cathy why this was inappropriate until she was blue in the face, but the child persisted in her loquacious ways. Mom asked how she could silence her daughter without stomping on her spirit.

I told Mom what she had already unwittingly discovered: you cannot talk a child into behaving properly. Consequences stop misbehavior—consequences that children do not like. Here was a case of a child disobeying his parents (doing what he has been told, one time, not to do) and parents getting upset. As things stood, Chatty Cathy had no incentive to stop blabbing family business to anyone who would listen. Only when Cathy blabbed and *Cathy* got upset, would Cathy stop blabbing.

I recommended a proactive, "strike while the iron is cold" approach. I'll let Cathy's mom describe what she did and the outcome in her own words:

My husband and I came up with a plan, then I talked to our daughter. I said, "This is embarrassing for all of us, and I've noticed that it's frustrating for you when we end up having to talk with you afterward about things that you should not have said." She agreed with me. She also said (and my jaw just about dropped at this one), "I know you and Dad know what's best for me, and I know that you wouldn't do anything on purpose to embarrass or hurt me." I told her that from that point on whenever she was with her dad or me while we were speaking to another adult, and she started to "contribute" to the conversation and then begin saying too much, we would quietly say, "My, we're talkative today." At that point she was to stop talking right away and say a phrase we agreed upon. She chose, "Well, I guess I'm done."

I told her that if she didn't stop talking after we mentioned the "secret code" phrase that she would end up spending time in her room and we would take away some privileges. I also told her that if she had any questions about things she heard during adult conversation, she could ask us questions later and we would decide what was appropriate to tell an eight-year-old.

Well, it didn't take long. In fact, the very next day, while I was speaking to another mom, Cathy started in. Immediately, I said, "My, we're talkative today." The other mom smiled and Cathy looked up at me with wide eyes. Then, without missing a beat, she said, "Well, I guess I'm done."

Later on we talked about what happened. I told her I appreciated her quick response to the matter. She said that by listening to us talk, she had learned a couple of things she didn't know before. I replied, "Well, it is important to listen carefully. That's why I've told you God gave us two ears and one mouth, because listening is more important than talking."

Well, John, since then we have only had to give her the secret code once. I'm a bit amazed, frankly, that a problem that's been so long in the making was solved so quickly.

This very inspirational story illustrates several important disciplinary principles:

1. Effective discipline is not primarily a matter of how you punish, but primarily a matter of how you communicate. Note, Mom stopped nagging and explaining and simply laid down the law.
2. Having a plan is essential to good discipline. Before, when daughter began blabbing, Mom reacted. To put an end to the problem, she and her husband came up with a plan and communicated it to their daughter. A reactive response is almost always emotional; therefore, reactivity is not authoritative. Proactivity ensures a much more authoritative response when misbehavior occurs.
3. In order to work, consequences must be consequential. Nagging is not consequential. Having freedom and privileges curtailed is consequential.
4. Last, but not least, consistency is vital. Note that Mom did exactly what she told her daughter she was going to do. She never deviated one iota from the plan.

Communication, consequences, consistency: that's what discipline is all about. That's not complicated at all, is it?

CHAPTER SIX

Seven Final Words of Advice

Parents who raise well-behaved children don't do so by accident. They didn't simply win the kid lottery. Nor do they have well-behaved kids because they master various discipline strategies. By and large, the fact that they have well-behaved kids can't be attributed to one single thing; nor can it be taken out of context. These parents create their own good fortune. They embody certain qualities and they create family environments that contain certain attributes. They are what I call Foundational Parents because they seem to understand, intuitively, that good behavior develops within a very specific set of conditions. Without that prerequisite foundation, the best discipline plan will flop. This chapter lays out the building blocks of that important family foundation.

PARENT THROUGH LEADERSHIP

Effective parenting is about leadership, not relationship. Leadership is the horse; relationship is the cart. It will follow in its time.

When I'm speaking to teachers on the issue of classroom discipline, I always ask, "Think about a teacher you know who always has the most orderly class, no matter what students she is assigned: is she using behavior modification methods to create a well-disciplined class environment?"

The answer, of course, is no. She is projecting proper leadership qualities, the qualities I identified in chapter 2. She projects a calm, casual authority to her students. Her leadership is what causes them to pay attention. They know that she has something to offer that will improve their lives, so they respect her and they obey her. She has a vision. She acts like she knows what she's doing, where she's going, and what she wants. She also acts like she knows that her students, with rare exception, are going to give her what she wants. Her students, in turn, know that what she wants is what's best for *them*.

I then ask, "Is that teacher trying to be liked by her students?" The answer is no.

And then, "Do her students like her?" The answer is yes.

Over the years, personal and professional experience with families has constantly strengthened my belief that the most well-behaved kids come from homes where parents are comfortable in their authority. If that doesn't describe you, you're hardly alone. Most of today's parents do not qualify. Most parents are trying to be liked by their kids. That disqualifies. Most parents consciously try not to make decisions that they know will cause their children to become upset. That disqualifies. Most parents—especially moms—would describe themselves as frequently stressed-out and anxious. That disqualifies. Most of today's parents get into regular arguments with their children. That disqualifies. The folks who qualify as Leadership Parents don't try to be liked, don't care that their kids don't like some of their decisions (but they certainly understand), would not say that raising kids is stressful, and will not enter into arguments with their kids.

These qualities are not elusive butterflies. If you don't possess them, then all you have to do is claim them as your prerogative and practice being the parent you want to be. Remember, it's not about your child's behavior as much as it is about *your* point of view. Your point of view determines how you react to your child and, therefore, it also has great influence over how your child reacts to you. Your point of view determines whether parenting stresses you out or not. Your point of view determines whether you get into arguments with your child or not. Successful parenting is not a matter of collecting lots of techniques and methods. It starts with the right point of view, which can be summarized simply: *Children do not know how to run their own lives competently. You are the parent. Your job is to manage their lives competently. If they don't agree with the way you are managing, well, that's too bad. Parenting and popularity are not synonymous.* Stay the course. They'll get it eventually.

CREATE A PARENT-CENTERED FAMILY

*The center of attention in a family ought to be
clearly occupied by adults or an adult.*

I helped raise two children into successful adulthoods, during which I spent a lot of time trying to figure out how to be a good father. I finally realized that I was barking up the wrong tree. I realized that a good husband is a good father, but it doesn't necessarily work the other way around—a good father is not always a good husband. Likewise, a good wife is always the best mother she is capable of being, but again, it doesn't necessarily work the other way around. The marriage came first; keep it first, and it will be much more likely to last.

So, the obvious question becomes: how does one translate this to single parenthood? I am qualified to speak on that because my mother was a single parent for most of the first seven years of my life. During that time I was blessed to have a mom who did *not* put me at the center of her attention, who did *not* burden me with the responsibility of being her primary relationship. Her life was filled with relationships: her siblings, her mother, and lots of friends. Her life was good; therefore, I felt a sense of well-being. I look back on that experience and realize that Mom gave me the greatest of all gifts: permission to grow up and away from her. She loved me, but she did not *need* me in her life. Therefore, I was free to eventually leave, without regret.

Married or single, parents need to enjoy full, rich lives outside of their responsibilities toward their children. Married couples should take annual vacations without children. They should have weekly date nights. They should put children to bed early so they can have some time with just one another. Married and single parents should have hobbies, individual pursuits, friends, interests, and the like that take them outside the home, away from children, into the world. All too often, the social life of today's parents is limited to other parents with children the same ages who are in the same activities. That's fine as far as it goes, but if that describes a parent's *entire* social life, that parent needs to find time away from the roles of mommy or daddy.

The more interesting your life, the more interesting you will be to your children; the more they will respect you, the more they will pay attention to you, and the easier parenting will be.

ASSIGN CHORES

Create a contributing role for each of your children
by assigning daily chores beginning at age three.

When all is said and done, the purpose of raising a child is to help the child out of your life and into a successful life of his or her own. Furthermore, the sooner that happens, the better for all concerned. I'm not suggesting that you kick your children out when they're fifteen or some such thing, of course. But I am saying that it's your job to help your children acquire the qualities and skills they will need to make the most of life and liberty, so they can pursue their own happiness successfully. In other words, it is your job, first and foremost, to raise a good citizen who loves God and his neighbors.

A good citizen-neighbor is a person who is willing to serve, to make a contribution. In fact, a good citizen-neighbor looks for opportunities to serve. It's important, therefore, that you teach your children that service is a virtue. Since all valuable lessons are first learned in the home, you can do just that by giving your children the opportunity to serve within your family by doing regular chores. Chores help children understand that in a free society, everyone must pull together, not to mention in the same general direction. They also teach responsibility and help children acquire a good work ethic.

"So we should pay for chores just like adults are paid for their work, right?" parents ask.

No, you should not pay for chores. Chores are service. When you pay for chores, they are no longer acts of service. Furthermore, you create the impression that if your child doesn't really need any money that week, he really doesn't have to do his chores. That's not what a good work ethic is all about. A good work ethic is going beyond the job description. It's about doing not just what you *have* to do, but also what you don't have to do but *needs* to be done.

In too many of today's families, children are consuming goods and resources, but they are not making a contribution that even begins to balance their consumption. That will eventually handicap their ability to be good citizen-neighbors. A viable culture depends more on contribution than on consumption. Give each of your kids a clearly defined role in your family. Start assigning chores when a child reaches age three and gradually expand his role and responsibilities from there. It will do all of us a world of good if you do. If you are interested in learning more about chores, how to organize them, how to manage them, and what chores are appropriate at what ages, see my book *A Family of Value.*[1] It contains an entire chapter devoted to those very issues.

PUT "TEAM FAMILY" FIRST

Maximize your family by keeping
extracurricular activities to a minimum.

In a given year, I am sure that I talk directly—either face-to-face, over the phone, by e-mail, or through my Web site—to more parents about parenting matters than any other individual in America, perhaps the world. I guess that makes me a World Champion Talking-to-Parents Guy. These contacts and conversations help me keep my finger on the pulse of contemporary parenting. As a consequence, I have a sense of what's working and what's not. One of the things I'm convinced isn't working is the emphasis currently placed on extracurricular activities.

I don't think anyone has ever done a time study of this issue, but I'll bet that if someone did, they'd discover that American parents are spending more time carting kids to and from and watching them perform in extracurricular activities than they are spending on any other parenting task. Is this time paying off? The usual justifications are that (a) the kids enjoy their activities, (b) they teach kids how to be team players, and (c) they help kids become well rounded.

To the first justification—"kids enjoy them"—I say, so what? Do adults get to do everything they enjoy doing? No. Why then should children get to do everything they enjoy doing? If anything, children need to learn that you don't ever in life get to do *everything* you enjoy doing. For example, I love deep-water fishing, golf, and listening to classic rock at full volume. Because of my responsibilities, I rarely get to indulge my passions. I can't even play my car CD player at full volume for fear I'll miss an important phone call. So I hardly play it at all. Yet I'm still a happy camper!

To the second justification—"these activities teach kids to be team players"—I say simply, hogwash. The greatest team of all is Team Family. Let's face it, folks: these extracurricular activities are consuming many families, body and soul. The kids in these consumed families may be learning how to play on a baseball team, but they need to learn how to be members of Team Family. Besides which, these after-school activities are preventing children from learning how to make decisions, solve problems, do for themselves. How so? Because these activities are micromanaged by well-meaning adults, that's how so. Adults make the decisions, solve the problems, and do, do, do for the kids. This is not a formula for growing up.

I talk to parents who don't have their kids in after-school activities. These are parents who believe it's more important that a family have a relaxed evening meal together, every evening, than it is for Little Johnny and Little Susie to be playing soccer or learning gymnastics. (Mind you, there's nothing wrong with soccer, gymnastics, or any of the other extra-curricular things children do. There is, however, something wrong with the level of adult overinvolvement in most of these things, and there is something definitely wrong when these after-school activities dominate the life of a family.) These outside-the-mainstream parents tell me that their Johnnies and Susies don't seem to be suffering from this "neglect." Quite the contrary, they consistently tell me that their families are more peaceful, less stressed, and that their kids have figured out creative ways of filling their discretionary time. I am a firm believer that what kids figure out for themselves in that regard will almost always be better by a long shot than what adults figure out for them.

I also feel that this whole concept of "well-rounded" is overblown. My sense is that today's parents think "well-rounded" consists of learning a little bit of this and a little bit of that, and so on. That is certainly not the definition of fifty-plus years ago when the term meant that an individual was well educated and could therefore carry on intelligent conversation, possessed good manners, and was comfortable and therefore gracious in any social setting. In the classical sense of the term, "well-rounded" does not imply that the individual has acquired, however minimally in each case, a collection of various skills. Nor did it refer to a person's achievements. It was about social graces, which—dare I say?—today's children are lacking, generally. There are exceptions, of course, but anyone my age knows that the social graces are not being adequately taught by most parents, and the observation is independent of parental demographics.

HELP YOUR KIDS DEVELOP HOBBIES

Help your kids discover and develop interests that
have the potential of becoming lifelong pursuits.

One observation I have, confirmed by parents, is that today's child is either in lots of after-school activities or he is in very few after-school activities and he has one or two hobbies. I believe in hobbies. I think if kids knew the difference, they'd pick hobbies too.

Hobbies can be lifelong pursuits. There will come a point in a person's life when, for whatever reason, he can't play basketball any longer. But when he can no longer play athletic sports, he can still collect stamps, paint with watercolors, play the guitar, or travel. Hobbies also keep kids out from "underfoot." Almost invariably, the kid who complains of being bored, who expects his parents to entertain him, is a kid without a hobby.

To start your child in a hobby, begin by thinking of the hobbies you enjoyed as a kid. Don't force your own interests on your child, but your own enthusiasm can be infectious. Take your child to a hobby store and help him choose something he'd like to begin developing. The folks who run the store can be a great help in this regard. Most of the people who work in hobby stores are passionate about what they do, and they love providing guidance to children and helping them get off on the right foot.

Hobbies develop independence, self-reliance, creativity, imagination, problem solving, decision making, perseverance, patience, planning, prioritizing, attention span, self-control, and hand-eye coordination. In short, they strengthen in all manner of ways the things you want strengthened in your child. I've never heard of a study being done on this, but my experience leads me to believe, strongly, that kids with hobbies are much better behaved and do better in school.

By the way, watching television and playing video games are not hobbies. When you think of hobbies, think of another "H" word: hands. Hobbies involve the hands! Hobbies are not passive pursuits. They keep a child's mental juices flowing!

BANISH THE IDIOT BOXES

Keep television and video games to a minimum
(less than five hours a week, cumulatively) in your kids' lives, and
let your kids use computers only when absolutely necessary.

Believe it or not, there are lots of parents out there who are leading productive, well-informed lives, including raising lovely children who do not allow television or other electronic media to occupy a major role in their families. There are lots of parents out there who don't even have televisions in their homes! All of said parents, without exception, tell me the same thing: "This is the single best thing I've ever done for my marriage, my family, and my kids."

From their unanimous testimonies, I conclude that when "idiot boxes" and "boob tubes"—television, video games, computers—are not centerpieces in a family, the family works a whole lot better. There's more peace in the family, less distraction, more conversation, more "relationship" going on, less sibling conflict, less argument between parents and children, more overall cooperation on the part of children, and children play more creatively. I've never talked to a parent who made the decision to have a virtually electronics-free family (no television, no video games, and only essential computer usage) who said anything but it's the best decision they ever made for themselves and their kids.

Funny. When I say this to a group of parents, it never fails that someone tells me he can't do without television: it's how he keeps informed. I beg to differ—politely, of course. Television does not inform you. Television is about sound and sight bites. To fit the format of television, information is compressed into capsules and fed to the viewer. With rare exception, a person watching television does not get the big picture concerning anything that's happening in the world. The big picture is obtained, as always, by reading. And by the way, researchers have found that the more parents read, the better readers their children become. What better reason to put television on the sidelines in your family!

I can personally testify to the benefits of a no-television lifestyle. Willie and I discovered the joys of an electronics-free home in the late 1970s. Because of problems one of our kids was having in school, we eliminated television for nearly five years. The changes we saw were overwhelmingly positive. I've since done lots of research on the effects electronics are having on children and have discovered things that are downright chilling. For example, there's no doubt that electronics are shortening children's attention spans. There's no doubt that kids who spend significant time playing video games and watching television don't do as well in school, regardless of IQ. There's no doubt that kids who don't watch television, play video games, and use computers frequently are more emotionally "level" than kids who spend lots of time in those pursuits.

Germane to this discussion is the fear, expressed by many parents, that a child who does not learn to manipulate electronic media at an early age will forever be behind the technology curve. This is hogwash. This is propaganda. Scare tactics. There's no substance to this idea at all. It's like saying, "If we don't begin teaching our child to drive when he's three, he may never be a good driver."

Techies have consistently told me that because of constant advances in software, the computer of the not-too-distant future will be as user-friendly as today's GPS. Indeed, the cell phone I purchased in the fall of 2008 has a GPS program in it. Without ever reading the directions, I became an expert GPS operator in less than a week. I truly don't think that my skills are any less than those of a person who's been using GPS technology for the past five years. The same is true of computers and kids. Take two kids of equal ability born in 2009. Give one a computer at age three; give the second child a computer at age sixteen. That's the year 2025. I am assured by folks in the industry that the two kids will be equally adept at operating all the basic programs within a month. But I'll just bet that the child who didn't get a computer until age sixteen will be a better reader, have a longer attention span, and be more well-rounded in the traditional sense of the term.

MAKE PROVERBS 22:6 YOUR VISION STATEMENT

It's about your child's character, not his achievements;
manners, not skills. Besides, people of good character
figure out how to share their gifts with the rest of us.

Proverbs 22:6—"Train up a child in the way he should go, and when he is old he will not depart from it (NKJV)—does not, as some seem to think, promise a good outcome to good parenting. Remember the Jeremiah Principle (chapter 2)? Proverbs 22:6 says that parents should be guided by a vision. It is the centerpiece of a biblical point of view concerning children and child rearing.

When I ask parents to describe the adult they want their child to be when he is thirty years old, they almost always use words like *honest, compassionate, charitable, thrifty, well-mannered, responsible, caring,* and *loving.* Parents do not describe that adult child in terms of prestige, power, acquisitions, wealth, or achievement. They use words that describe desirable character traits. In effect, every parent's vision is to raise a child of good character—a good citizen-neighbor.

Every person in business, no matter what the pursuit, will tell you that in order for a business to operate smoothly, it must be guided by a mission statement. The mission statement is the company's vision. Your mission is to raise a child who will glorify God in everything he or she does and be a person of benefit to family, friends, community, and culture. Your mission is *not* to raise a computer whiz, a valedictorian, a professional athlete, a well-known entertainer, or a future president of the United States. If your child achieves one of those things, fine and dandy, but always be mindful of the fact that nothing is more valuable than honesty and compassion and thrift and the like. Nothing is of more value to an individual than good character, and nothing is more valuable to a culture than citizens of good character.

Unfortunately, all too many of today's parents, their good intentions aside, are seemingly focused primarily on helping their children achieve, in sports and in school and in other extracurricular activities like musical instrument lessons. Furthermore, they are unwittingly teaching their children that satisfaction in life is about acquisition. These same parents, mind you, would use character words to describe the adults they want their kids to be when they're thirty years old. They say one thing, they do another. These parents are not irresponsible by any means. Nor are they shallow materialists. They've just allowed themselves to be swept up in current child-rearing mania, the theme of which is "The Parents of the Highest Achieving Child Are the Best Parents!"

Can you teach good character, and if so, how? The answers are (a) yes, you can teach character, and (b) you do so primarily by teaching good manners. Good character is about paying attention to others and looking for opportunities to serve others. Good manners are demonstrations of paying attention to others and looking for opportunities to serve others. Good character is about respect for others. Good manners are demonstrations of respect for others.

It's quite simple, really. If you truly want to raise a child of good character (and you are willing to back off the achievement thing), then teach manners. Practice good table manners at your family dinner table (another reason why it's important to eat as many meals as possible at your own dinner table). Rehearse good manners with your children before going into social situations. Every week, focus on and practice the "Manner of the Week."

Mind you, good manners do not stop with "thank you" and not reaching across the table for the salt shaker. Good manners are more than just not being rude and not offending others. They are about being helpful. They are about service. Teach your kids to open doors for people, to pick things up that others have dropped, to offer to carry things for people. Teach your children to pay attention to others and ask themselves, "What can I do, right now, to make this person more comfortable?"

By teaching good manners, you ensure that your children's esteem for others will be higher than their self-esteem. This is good. Believe it or not (and this is hard for today's parents to believe, for sure), researchers have found that people with high self-esteem lack regard for others. It appears to be what's called a zero-sum relationship. As esteem for the self—the toddler's Almighty Me—goes up, esteem for others goes down. I will propose that culture is strengthened *not* by people with high esteem for themselves, but by people who pay attention to and look for opportunities to serve others. Agree? Of course you do!

"But John!" someone may protest. "I want my child to possess self-confidence!" Let us not confuse our terms here. The research has found that these are not synonymous. In fact, there is no evidence that people who are humble and modest lack the belief that they are capable of dealing adequately with life's challenges. But there is lots and lots of evidence to the effect that people with high self-esteem consistently overestimate their abilities. For this reason, people with high self-esteem are *more* likely to experience disappointment and feelings of failure than people who are humble and modest. In other words, people with high self-esteem are more prone to becoming depressed than people who are humble and modest.

Because of secular-progressive propaganda to the effect that high self-esteem is something no one should do without, you may be struggling intellectually with what I've said in the last two paragraphs. But your common sense knows that what I've said is true. Let me help you awaken your common sense by asking you a few questions: Would you rather that your best friend have high self-esteem or be humble and modest? Would you rather that your employer have high self-esteem or be humble and modest? Would you rather that your spouse have high self-esteem or be humble and modest?

Really? Fancy that!

The good neighbor, the good citizen, is humble and modest. That's been known for thousands of years. What better authority on the subject than Jesus? He did not say, "Blessed are those who think highly of themselves." Hardly. He blessed the meek, the poor in spirit, those who mourn, and so on (Matthew 5:3–5). He blessed those who *don't* think highly of themselves—the humble. Paraphrasing Isaiah, Jesus said, "And whoever exalts himself will be humbled, and he who humbles himself will be exalted" (Matt. 23:12; Isaiah 2:11).

Do all you can to prevent your child from ever exalting himself. You can begin by not exalting your child. Teach him good manners. Make every effort to help him become well-rounded, in the classical sense of the term. Make Team Family the number one priority in your, and his, life.

And always keep your eyes fixed on the mission. Stay on course. Make Proverbs 22:6 your parenting mantra.

Read This Last!

Your grandmother could have written this book. She could have written all of my books, in fact. The stuff I tell parents is not new. I do not believe there is anything new under the sun. The belief that, because times have changed, we need to change how we raise kids has wreaked havoc in the family, the school, and culture.

But it's not too late to save the day. If it was, I'd stop doing what I'm doing, join a rock-and-roll band, and have lots of fun. I'm having fun as it is, mind you, but I'm a man on a mission. I absolutely know that the Big Guy gave me an assignment, and I have no choice but to do what He tells me to do. I've had my fill of disobedience.

My mission, as grandiose as it may sound, is to help American parents (a) understand that they have been misled by the psychobabblers and (b) get back on the right track as concerns the all-important, culture-building responsibility of raising children, the next generation. Will the next generation improve America or continue its decline into decadence?

The most important chapters in this book are chapters 1, 2, and 6.

They are foundational, and every project depends on solid foundations. For many parents, however and unfortunately, the primary appeal of this book will be chapters 3, 4, and 5. Today's parents want to know what to *do*. They're impatient. They want to cut to the chase. They can't wait. That's why I stressed in "Read This First!" the importance of not going straight to the methodologies set forth in those chapters.

The problems in American parenting, the problems with the behavior of so many American children, are not going to be solved by methods. They did not come about because of wrong methods, and they are not going to be solved by right ones. These problems came about because American parents were persuaded, by the psychobabblers (who began coming on the scene in the late 1960s and have been babbling ever since) to change their way of thinking about children and child rearing. This change of thinking was reflected by a new word: *parenting*. The word itself makes it sound as though raising children is a technology. It's not surprising, then, that so many parents believe in discipline technologies— time-out, logical and natural consequences, star charts, and the like.

But if the problems came about because of a change of thinking— from right thinking to wrong thinking—then the problems can only be solved by parents who begin to think right again. This book, therefore, is an attempt on my part (to paraphrase Bob Dylan) to "change your way of thinking," to help you acquire a different set of rules. Read chapters 1, 2, and 6 again. Those are the crux of this book. The methodologies set forth in chapters 3, 4, and 5 are simply examples of how to translate your new way of thinking into practice.

The crux of your new way of thinking is the understanding that parenting is leadership. Leadership is not a technology. It's a matter of presentation, of carrying one's authority with complete confidence in the rightness of one's mission. You don't have to justify your authority to your children: your authority was assigned to you by God. You don't need to justify your decisions to your children.

The headmaster of a private school in Virginia told an audience of parents that he had recently been informed that most of the seventh graders didn't agree with something he had said during a student assembly. He said, "I was glad to hear that."

Leaders *have* to make unpopular decisions. And once having made a decision, however unpopular, a leader must stay the course. He must say what he means and mean what he says. His "yes" must mean nothing short of "yes," and his "no" must mean nothing but "no" (see Matthew 5:37).

The seventh, and presumably last, "word of advice" I set forth in chapter 6 is an encouragement to parents to make Proverbs 22:6 their parenting vision statement. Actually, I have an eighth word of advice: Love your children enough to raise them according to the first seven.

May your child rearing be blessed by the peace of the Lord.

—John Rosemond
May 18, 2009

Notes

Read This First!
1. To be honest, I can't prove beyond a shadow of doubt that these are the seven most common issues, but they are the top seven behavior problems parents ask me about.
2. John Rosemond, *Making the Terrible Twos Terrific!* (Kansas City, MO: Andrews McMeel, 1993).
3. John Rosemond, *Teen-Proofing* (Kansas City, MO: Andrews McMeel, 2000).

Chapter 1
1. Adele Faber and Elaine Mazlish, *How to Talk So Kids Will Listen & Listen So Kids Will Talk* (New York: Rawson Association, 1980).
2. Kevin Leman, *Have a New Kid by Friday!* (Grand Rapids: Revell, 2008).

Chapter 2
1. Behavior modification may *appear* to work in very specific, contrived situations (e.g., residential rehabilitation programs for incorrigible teenagers), but evidence of wider effectiveness is lacking.

2. For more on this, read *The Diseasing of America's Children* (Nashville: Thomas Nelson, 2008), written by yours truly with pediatrician Dr. Bose Ravenel.

3. It is a given that parents who read parenting books love their children unconditionally; therefore, we can bypass the topic of unconditional love and move on to the issue of leadership.

4. Some other options for letting your child know who's boss are: "Because I'm the mom," "Because I'm in charge," "Because that's my decision," or simply, "You must obey."

5. Other equally suitable names are the Chair of My Final Answer or the Chair of Perpetual Prohibition. The idea behind the name is that the child becomes wise to the fact that you're not going to change your mind.

6. Again, see *The Diseasing of America's Children* for the exposé on this fiction.

7. Read more on this in chapter 3.

Chapter 3

1. Tickets are easier to handle and more durable if laminated, which can be accomplished with self-laminating film bought at any craft store or most superstores, like Wal-mart or Target.

2. If you don't spend most of your time at home near the kitchen (for example, if your playroom is upstairs and your kitchen downstairs), you can hang your Target Misbehavior List somewhere that's readily available and where you spend most of your time.

3. Milton H. Erickson, Ernest L. Rossi, Sheila I. Rossi, *Hypnotic Realities: The Induction of Clinical Hypnosis and Forms of Indirect Suggestion* (New York: Irvington, 1976).

Chapter 4

1. Burton L. White, *The First Three Years of Life* (New Jersey: Prentice Hall, 1975).

2. All over America, physicians and mental health professionals are telling parents this sort of stuff about this supposed condition they call "early-onset bipolar disorder." The truth, the whole truth, and nothing but the truth is that no compelling objective evidence exists to support any of this stuff. No one has ever proven that a proclivity for

wild and unpredictable mood swings and tantrums is passed from family member to family member through genes. No one has ever proven that something called a "biochemical imbalance" even exists. This stuff is made up! Along with pediatrician Bose Ravenel, I've written an entire book on this fiction: *The Diseasing of America's Children: Exposing the ADHD Fiasco and Empowering Parents to Take Back Control* (Nashville: Thomas Nelson, 2008). I recommend you read it if someone has even *suggested* that your child has ADHD, oppositional defiant disorder, or EOBD.

Chapter 6

1. John Rosemond, *A Family of Value* (Kansas City, MO: Andrews McMeel, 1995).

Acknowledgments

I'm very grateful to my stalwart editors at Thomas Nelson, Deb Wickwire and Jenn McNeil; my even more stalwart wife of forty-one years, Willie; and the many parents and children whose stories fill these pages for helping me make this book happen.

About the Author

I n 1971, at the age of twenty-four, when whoever I am emerged from the safety of Western Illinois University, I'd been married to Willie for four years and was the father of Eric, then going on three. Shortly thereafter, Amy (Famous Amos) came along. I worked in various capacities in various community mental health centers and one small liberal arts college until 1980, when I entered private practice. My first book was published in 1989, and it's been a very interesting ride since then. I became a true believer in my Lord and Savior Jesus Christ about ten years ago, and the ride became even more interesting. "Born again" equals a completely different perspective that becomes more clear with nearly every passing day. My mission—and therefore my books, columns, talks, and the way I counsel—has slowly changed since then as I shed the old and take on the new. Willie and I have lived in Gastonia, North Carolina, since 1976. Eric and Amy, their spouses, and our seven grand grandchildren live within close proximity. What more could a guy ask for? I truly hope you enjoy and that your family profits greatly from this book.

My website is www.rosemond.com.

JUST RELEASED! John Rosemond's brand-new DVD series, "The Well-Behaved Child: The Keys to Effective Discipline," a perfect video supplement to *The Well Behaved Child: Discipline that REALLY Works!*

This 2-part, 160-minute interactive skillshop DVD based on the book provides parents with the information and skills they need to begin making significant positive changes in their discipline style and, therefore, their children's behavior.

As usual, John laces his presentation before a live audience with humor, and plenty of it! Parents are sure to feel not only relieved of significant guilt and anxiety, but also inspired, informed, and ready to become calm, self-confident leaders of children.

Visit John's online bookstore at
www.rosemond.com for more information.

PARENTS, TEACHERS, AND EVEN PROFESSIONALS ARE BEING DECEIVED ABOUT ADHD!

The Diseasing of America's Children empowers parents to take back control of their children by recognizing the misinformation they have been given and applying a commonsense, traditional approach to managing their children's behavior problems. With candor and insight, Rosemond and Ravenel draw upon verifiable scientific research and their years of professional experience to outline proven parenting methods that will help even the most difficult children to behave functionally at home and school—without medical intervention.

Available wherever books are sold.

FAMILY PSYCHOLOGIST JOHN ROSEMOND

is America's busiest and most popular speaker on parenting issues. In a typical year, he is invited to give some two hundred presentations and workshops to parent, teacher, professional, and corporate groups across the USA. John has also spoken in England, Belgium, Mexico, Canada, the Caribbean, Turkey, and Spain.

"I was utterly riveted by this seminar and have talked non-stop to other parents about it! I feel I have a lot of solid techniques to use at home, but the greatest gift is the empowerment I feel as a parent."
—RM/Columbia, SC/April 2009

"This was not only immensely enjoyable, but will also benefit me greatly both as a parent and as a family physician!"
—Dr. P/Atlanta, GA/March 2008

To obtain more information about John's seminars,
including his availability, go to the Seminars and Workshops page at
www.rosemond.com.